"All My Trials, Lord"

"ALL MY TRIALS, LORD"

Selections from Women's Slave Narratives

by Mary Young

The African-American Experience
FRANKLIN WATTS
A Division of Grolier Publishing
New York / London / Hong Kong / Sydney
Danbury, Connecticut

Library of Congress Cataloging-in-Publication Data

Contents

〰️

Acknowledgments

A project of this type could not be carried out without the help of many people, including Susan Figge, the Dean of the Faculty of The College of Wooster, who financed research at the Schomberg Library. A special thanks to Barbara Hampton of The College of Wooster, who as usual gave structure and organization to a rambling manuscript, and to my family, who always support me.

"All My Trials, Lord"

Introduction

~⬙~

Although the first slave narrative—that of Brittin Hammon—was published in Boston as early as 1768, the overwhelming number of narratives were published between the years 1830 and 1860, and were immensely important to the cause of the abolitionists. Until the appearance of the slave narratives, almost all public discussions of slavery in the United States were conducted solely from the perspectives of whites. In the slave narratives, however, blacks were able to participate in the national discussion on slavery for the first time and present slavery from the perspective of the enslaved man and woman. A brilliant and often unforgiving light illuminates the horror of slavery in these accounts. Not surprisingly, the abolitionists considered the publication of slave narratives as one of the most potent weapons in the campaign to turn popular opinion against this evil.

Slave narratives attempted to describe as accurately as possible, without exaggeration, the true conditions of slavery as experienced by the authors. The emphasis on the truth in these narratives promoted a radical debate on slavery, undermining the slaveholders' defense of slavery.

Narratives of slave women compose less than twelve percent of the more than six thousand narratives in existence; yet this in no way precludes their equal importance. Although the inhumanity of enslavement was common to the experiences of both men and women, there was a difference particular to the women's suffering—the sexual exploitation of the female slave. Harriet Jacobs's *Incidents in the Life of A Slave Girl* is one of a few narratives that candidly discuss the issue of sexual exploitation. Jacobs, like many slave mothers, is also outraged at the thought that her daughter will inherit her condition and be subject to the same fate. A great fear and sorrow of slave mothers was that their daughters would also be slaves.

A cardinal rule of slave owners had been that slave women must never reveal the paternity of their mulatto children, a silence that enabled slave owners to hide their practice of fathering their own slaves. To explain the presence of biracial slaves, the slave owners had created a mythology about the immorality of black women and the purity of white women. But through their narratives, slave women were able to reveal the truth. Portrayals of the exploitation of female slaves by the white slave owner and the heartbreaking disruption of families was a unique contribution of the women's slave narratives.

CHRONOLOGICAL DEVELOPMENT
Perhaps the earliest surviving slave narrative of an African-American woman can be found in the seventeenth-century history of Alice that appeared in

Isaiah Thomas's *Eccentric Biography; or, Memoirs of Remarkable Female Characters, Ancient and Modern,* first published in 1803. Alice was born into slavery in Philadelphia in 1686 of parents who had been shipped from Barbados. She never sued for her freedom, but she was known as an unusually independent and resourceful person. Laboring as a ferrywoman,* which gave her a certain amount of freedom, Alice was honest, responsible, and tactful. She was ". . . so careful to keep the truth, that her veracity was never questioned; her honesty also was unimpeached, for such was her master's confidence in it, that she was trusted at all times to receive the ferriage 'money for upwards of forty years." Alice witnessed the beginnings of the city of Philadelphia and remembered the founder of Pennsylvania, William Penn. She died in 1802 in Bristol, Pennsylvania, at the age of 116.†

In 1783, at the age of seventy, Belinda, "an African" of Boston, petitioned the Massachussetts court for an allowance from the estate of her former owner, Isaac Royal, who had fled the American colonies during the Revolutionary War and left her free to starve. The petition is a narrative that sketches her early years in Africa, where men "whose faces were like the moon" kidnapped her from her community's sacred grove with "Bows and Arrows [that] were like the thunder and lightning of the Clouds."‡ On the slave ship were ". . . three hundred Africans in chains, suffering the most excruciating torments, and some of them rejoicing

---

*A Woman who keeps, looks after, or operates a ferry.
†Sidney Kaplan, *The Black Presence in the Era of the American Revolution, 1770–1800* (Amherst: University of Massachusetts, 1973).
‡Ibid., p. 214

that the pangs of death came like balm to their wound."* Belinda's petition to the court attempted to hold the young United States government to its declaration of the individual's right to life, liberty, and the pursuit of happiness. She was demanding her payment for years of free labor by requesting a share of her former owner's estate.

> The face of your petitioner, is now marked with the furrows of time, and her frame feebly bending under the oppression of years, while she, by the Laws of the Land, is denied the enjoyment of one morsel of that immense wealth, a part whereof hath been accumulated by her own industry, and the whole augmented by her servitude.†

Historian Sidney Kaplan speculates that another black person—possibly poet Phillis Wheatley or abolitionist and Masonic leader Prince Hall—served as the actual writer of the document. Whether Belinda wrote the petition herself is less important than the fact that her perspective was committed to paper and became a part of both American and African-American literary history. If she did not write the document herself, she provided the information that it contained, and by her mark she assumed responsibility for it.

The greatest number of slave narratives were published between 1830 and 1860, coinciding with the rise of the abolitionist movement. The narratives were effective weapons in the war against slavery and were much used by the movement.

Following emancipation there was a drop-off in

*Ibid.
†Ibid., p. 215.

the publication of slave narratives. Toward the end of the nineteenth century, however, narratives recurred in the form of reminiscences. Some daughters of former slaves wrote and published their mothers' stories; other women remembered slavery and wanted to tell their own stories.

In the 1930s, interest in the slave narratives again revived. The John B. Cade collection consists of eighty-two narratives of ex-slaves who were interviewed by thirty-six students under Cade's direction. These narratives, which were collected in 1929 in Louisiana, are housed in Southern University, Scotlandville, Louisiana.

The Reddick Collection contains 260 unpublished narratives of ex-slaves who were interviewed by twelve graduate students working under the guidance of Dr. L. D. Reddick. These narratives, which were collected in 1934–35 from persons in the five states bordering the Ohio River, are in the Schomberg Collection of the New York Public Library.

In 1936, during the Great Depression, a project was begun to collect the testimony of ex-slaves. Unemployed writers and researchers hired by the Works Progress Administration (WPA) used a set of questions to interview ex-slaves about their experiences. More than two thousand former slaves were questioned as part of the program. At the time, not many former slaves remained and researchers realized it was crucial to capture their memories for posterity.

There are many unexamined narratives in collections around the country: in The Library of Congress' Collection on Slavery, the State University of Ohio, the Newberry Library in Chicago, Wellesley College in Massachusetts, and Fisk University in Tennessee.

Belinda Hurmence has edited eleven women's narratives in *My Folks Don't Want Me to Talk About Slavery: Twenty-one Oral Histories of Former North Carolina Slaves,* that chronicle tales of cruelty, injustice, and abuse.

In the 1970s the revitalized women's movement generated interest in the history and writings of women. Works by rediscovered women writers were reprinted, among which were women's slave narratives. Marian Wilson Starling has done groundbreaking work on slave narratives. In *The Slave Narrative: Its Place in American History* (1988), she meticulously examines and analyzes approximately six thousand narratives from different periods.

FORM OF THE SLAVE NARRATIVE

Slave narratives were produced in three ways. Some narratives were authored by the slave herself—for example, Harriet Jacobs's *Incidents in the Life of A Slave Girl.* But literacy was something withheld from most slaves, and therefore many slaves could not write their own stories. Numerous narratives were dictated to another person—for example, the narrative of Harriet Tubman. The narratives often document the achievement of literacy, which was treasured as much as freedom. Slaveholders and other whites assumed unlettered slaves to be ignorant and easily dominated. So insistent were the owners on slave illiteracy that southern laws specifically prohibited slaves, under penalty of death, from learning to read and write. Uneducated slaves could not, after all, write their own passes. Besides, slaves who could not read could not challenge their owners' explanation of the Scriptures, which were used to justify slavery as God's will. A third method of producing the slave

16

narrative was the interview—as found in the narrative of Louisa Picquet.

The slave narratives included a search for identity and humanity; a confirmation of the power of religion; a motif of the journey, both physical and psychological; the importance of self-reliance and bonding; and the value of community. But always the story told of the escape from bondage to freedom.

Religion was important in the lives of both slave men and women. Narratives of religous conversion center on the importance of Christianity in the lives of the enslaved African. Sometimes in women's narratives, there is a focus on the actions of men who tried to prevent women from preaching the word of God. An example of the conversion narrative is Zilpha Elaw's *Memoirs of the Life, Religious Experience, Ministerial Travels and Labours of Mrs. Zilpha Elaw, An American Female of Color; Together with Some Account of the Great Religious Revivals in America* (1846) and *Jarena Lee's Religious Experiences and Journal of Jarena Lee, Giving an Account of Her Call to Preach the Gospel* (1849). Many such narratives are still being discovered. In 1981, Jean McMahon Humez edited the collected writings of Rebecca Cox Jackson, *Gifts of Power: The Writings of Rebecca Jackson, Black Visionary, Shaker Eldress.*

THE LITERARY IMPORTANCE
OF THE SLAVE NARRATIVE

In addition to the effect on the struggle to end slavery, the slave narratives have greatly influenced the works of black authors and white authors. In the nineteenth century the accounts written by ex-slaves were so popular that many writers used the form for their fiction. Several nineteenth-century novels used a form that is similar to the structure of the slave narrative. William Wells Brown (1816–1884)—ex-slave, abolitionist, and long considered the first African-American novelist—published *Clotelle, or the President's Daughter* in 1853. Brown used many details covered in his own slave narrative, *The Narrative of William Wells Brown* (1847). He presents all the evils of slavery, including enslaved Africans running away and then being hunted by vicious dogs. Additionally, he exploits much unsubstantiated historical gossip, as for example, Thomas Jefferson's alleged long liaison with a slave woman, Sally Hemmings. Brown also uses folklore and other aspects of slave life, such as quadroon balls and the doctoring of slaves for market. Some critics believe the book was written for a primarily white audience because Brown portrays dark-skinned blacks as less intelligent than light-skinned blacks.

White writers in the nineteenth century also used the slave narrative form. Mark Twain's *The Adventures of Huckleberry Finn* (1883), one of the greatest American novels, has a young white boy, Huck, and a runaway slave, Jim, as its heroes.

Other nineteenth-century writers also used the form. Richard Hildreth, a historian, supposedly produced the first antislavery novel, *Archy Moore, The White Slave, or Memoirs of a Fugitive*. The novel was first published anonymously in 1836. In 1856, twenty-five years after Nat Turner's slave revolt in Virginia, Hildreth admitted authorship and enlarged and republished his novel as *The White Slave*. The novel concerns Archy's fight against bondage and his final escape to freedom.

Perhaps the most famous popular novel to use the slave narrative form is Harriet Beecher Stowe's *Uncle Tom's Cabin* (1852). According to legend, when Abraham Lincoln met Stowe, he said, "So this is the little lady who wrote the book that started the war."

In the twentieth century white writers continued the use of the slave narrative: Robert Penn Warren, *Band of Angels* (1955), and William Styron, whose *The Confessions of Nat Turner,* an imagined portrayal of the historical black revolutionary, won the Pulitzer Prize in 1967.

As for the twentieth-century black writers, those participating in the Harlem Renaissance (1916–1929), or the New Negro Movement, as it was also known, turned to black folklore for inspiration. The use of the slave narrative continued in James Weldon Johnson's *The Autobiography of an Ex-Colored Man* (1912). This search for a usable past went on with Arna Bontemps (1902–1973) and *Black Thunder* (1936); Richard Wright (1908–1960), *Black Boy* (1945); Ralph Ellison (1914–1994), *Invisible Man* (1952); and William Melvin Kelley (1937–), *In A Different Drummer* (1969). Also using this tradition is Ishmael Reed's comedic *Flight to Canada* (1976), David Bradley's *The Chaneysville Incident* (1981), and Charles Johnson's *Oxherding Tale* (1982).

So too have black women writers incorporated the structure of the narratives into their writings: for example, Frances Harper in *Iola Leroy, or Shadows Uplifted*; Pauline Hopkins in *Contending Forces*; and Zora Neale Hurston in *Their Eyes Were Watching God.*

Margaret Walker (1915–) published her novel *Jubilee,* the story of her great-grandmother, Vyry, in 1966. Vyry's story had been the subject of Walker's doctoral dissertation at the University of Iowa. As a novel, *Jubilee* won the Houghton Mifflin Literary Award in 1966. Shirley Anne Williams, like Margaret Walker, created a neonarrative, a new form of the slave narrative, with her novel, *Dessa Rose* (1986). Octavia Butler also uses elements of the narrative in her science fiction, for example, in *Kindred* (1979).

Perhaps the most striking use of the slave narrative is found in *Beloved* by Toni Morrison. *Beloved* explores outraged motherhood and the shocking lengths to which an ex-slave mother will go to prevent her daughter from being returned to slavery. In 1994 Toni Morrison was awarded the Nobel Prize for Literature.

A Woman in Hiding

This excerpt about a woman slave—which is found in the slave narrative *Life and Adventures of Robert. The Hermit of Massachusetts*, by Henry Trumbull, published in 1829—is presented in its entirety.[1]

> The heart would sicken at the recital of the punishments inflicted upon and the extreme sufferings of the unhappy slaves of the south—indeed so goarding [sic] is the yoke of bondage, that while some are driven to the desperate act of not only destroying their own lives, but that of their wretched offspring—others seek to obtain their freedom by secreting themselves in thick swamps and marshes; where they remain concealed until they either fall victims to, or are compelled by hunger to return again to their masters, and submit to the punishment which those unfeeling wretches deem the merited reward of their disobedience! A remarkable

instance of the latter occurred in the State of North Carolina about fourteen years ago, and although the particulars appeared in many of our public prints, at that time, yet as they may have escaped the notice of many of our readers, we have thought that it would not be improper to republish them—they are from the pen of a respectable gentleman of Petersburg, communicated to his friend in New York—they follow:

While I resided in Newbern, N.C., in 1814, being informed that a Negro woman and two small children, had been that day brought in, who had been runaways for several years, I felt a wish to go and see them particularly as there was something curious connected with their history. My friend accompanied me to the jail, for they had been lodged there for safe keeping. We there learned the particulars of the life which they lived, or rather the miserable existence which they dragged out, during the seven years which they had spent in the swamps in the neighborhood of Newbern.

The owner of the woman, about seven years previously, removed to the western country and carried with him all his slaves, except this woman and an infant girl, then in the arms of its mother who, rather than be separated from her husband, who was owned by another person, timely eloped with her child, and completely avoided the vigilance of her pursuers.

Those who are acquainted with the lower section of that state, well know that it abounds in marshes and fens over grown with weeds, and interspersed, in some places, with clumps of pine trees. In one of those dreary retreats this woman found means to conceal herself for the space of seven years: and to find means also for her subsistence, partly by her own exertions and the assistance of her husband, who would occasionally make her a visit. Living in this situation, she soon had an additional burden upon her hands by the birth of another child.

The manner in which she concealed herself as well as her children from the discovery, was truly singular. By the strictest discipline, she prevented them ever crying aloud; she compelled them to stifle their little cries and complaints, though urged to it by pinching hunger, or the severest cold. She prohibited them from speaking louder than a whisper. This may appear strange to relate, but it is certainly true; and as a proof that no deception was used in this case it was satisfactorily ascertained, that after they had remained in town for more than a month, in the company of children who were nosily and clamorous, they were not known in a single instance to raise their voices higher than a soft whisper. At first, it was with great difficulty that they could stand or walk erect, and when they did attempt to walk, it was with a low stoop, the bust inclining forward, and with a hasty step like a patridge [*sic*]. But their favorite position was that of squatting upon their hams. In this posture, they could remain for hours without any apparent weariness, and at a given signal would move one after the other with great facility, and at the same time with so much caution, that not the least noise could be heard of their footsteps.

Their method for subsistence was the most extraordinary; sometimes the husband, according to the woman's account would fail to bring them supplies; and whether the fear of detection prevented her from intruding on the rights of others, or whether she was prevented by conscientious motives is not for me to determine—but in support of herself and children, have recourse to expedients which nothing but the most pressing necessity could ever suggest.

Frogs and terrapins were considered as rare dainties, and even snakes would be taken as a lawful prize to satisfy the calls of hunger.—It was the custom, said the woman in the little family, when they made up a fire in the night, and this was done only in the cold nights of winter, for one to sit up, while the others slept. The one who watched had a double duty to perform— not only to do the ordinary duty of a centinel [*sic*], but to watch for mice; which they contrived in the following manner. The person watching, would spread a little meat on the ground, or a few grains of corn or peas, or for want of these, a crust of bread when they had it; over which an old handkerchief or piece of cloth, was spread, then, observing a profound and deathlike silence, the mice would creep from their retreats in order to possess themselves of the bait.—The centinel, true to his post, as soon as the cloth was moved by the vagrant mouse, would very dexterously smack down a pair of hand upon him, and secure him for purposes yet to be mentioned. The flesh, as may be supposed, was used for food, which they devoured with as little ceremony as a boy would eat a snow bird; but even the skin was not thrown away; for they being carefully preserved, the hair or fur was picked off and mixed with wool or cotton for the purpose of making gloves and stockings—and they managed to spin up the materials they could procure, by means of a stick about six or eight inches in length.—This was held in the left hand, while, with the right, they held the materials to be spun, they gave us a specimen of their adroitness in this art; and the little boy, who was not above five years old, could manage his stick with surprising dexterity.—Several pair of stockings and gloves were shown, which had been knit by these singular beings, during their voluntary banishment.—They were grotesque enough in their appearance, and were made up of a greater medley of materials than are generally used in the civilized world.

How much longer this deluded African, with her two wretched children, would have remained in the comfortless savannahs of North Carolina, is not known, had not the woman been deserted by her husband:—Being deprived of the solace she derived from his transient visits, and the scanty subsistence she received from his hand, her situation became miserable beyond description. At length emaciated with hunger she crept to the road, gave herself up, with her equally meager looking charges, to the first person she saw, who happened very fortunately to be a man, with his cart going towards town—the sight, indeed, to the citizen was a novel one, if we may judge from the number who crowded to see and determine for themselves.

Mary Prince

From *The History of Mary Prince, A West Indian Slave,* written by Herself, published in 1831.[2]

Although Mary Prince lived in the West Indies and was a British slave, her experiences were not very different from those of enslaved women in the United States. She was born at Brackish-Pond, Bermuda, on a farm owned by Charles Myners. Both her parents were slaves. Her father was a sawyer* who belonged to a shipbuilder, Mr. Trimmingham.

When Mary was an infant, Mr. Myners died and "Old Captain Darrel" bought Mary and her mother for his grandchild, Betsey Williams. For Mary, this was the happiest period of her life: ". . . I was too young to understand rightly my condition as a slave. . . ."

Her new owner was a seaman, "a very harsh, and selfish man; and we always dreaded his return from sea." His wife apparently enjoyed his absences as well because her behavior changed when he returned. This owner did not handle his finances

*A workman who saws timber

well, so when Mary was about twelve years old she was hired out to a Mrs. Pruden. While working for Mrs. Pruden, Mary learned to read and write.

> Directly she had said her lessons to her grandmamma, she [Fanny, Mrs. Pruden's grand-daughter] used to come running to me, and make me repeat them one by one after her; in a few months I was able not only to say many letters but to spell many small words.

[One day,]

> Mrs. Pruden came to me and said, "Mary, you will have to go home directly; your master is going to be married, and he means to sell you and two of your sisters to raise money for the wedding."

Captain Darrel took Mary, her mother, and her sisters, Hannah and Dinah, to the slave mart for the sale. It was a very emotional time for all.

> But who cared for that? Did one of the many by-standers, who were looking at us so careless, think of the pain that wrung the hearts of the negro women and her young ones? . . . They were not all bad, I dare say, but slavery hardens white people's hearts towards the blacks; and many of them were not slow to make their remarks upon us aloud, without regard to our grief—though their light words fell like cayenne* on the fresh wounds of our hearts. Oh, those white people have small hearts who can only feel for themselves.

At the auction, Mary was "surrounded by strange

*A hot red pepper.

27

men, who examined and handled me in the same manner that a butcher would a calf or a lamb he was about to purchase." As these men examined her body, they made crude remarks about her shape and size.

She was sold to a Captain I——, whose wife was a brutal, heartless woman who delighted in physically abusing her slaves. "To hang me up by the wrists and lay my flesh open with the cow-skin was an ordinary punishment for even a slight offence."

Finally Captain I—— sent Mary to Turk's Island to be sold, not even allowing her to say good-bye to her own family. "Oh, the Buckra [white] people who keep slaves think that black people are like cattle, without natural affection."

Mr. D——, one of the owners of a salt pond, bought her. ". . . He received a certain sum for every slave that worked upon his premises, whether they were young or old."

I was given a half barrel and a shovel, and had to stand up to my knees in the water from four o'clock in the morning till nine, when we were given some Indian corn boiled in water. . . . We were then called again to our tasks and worked through the heat of the day; the sun flaming upon our heads like fire, and raising salt blisters in those parts which were not completely covered. Our feet and legs, from standing in the salt water for so many hours, soon became full of dreadful boils, which eat down in some cases to the very bone, afflicting the sufferers with great torment. We came home at twelve; ate our corn soup, called blawly, as fast as we could, and went back to our employment till dark at night. We then shovelled up the salt in

large heaps, and went down to the sea where we
washed the pickle from our limbs, and cleaned
the barrows and shovels from the salt.

Mary worked at Turk's Island for ten years until
Mr. D——retired to his home in Bermuda. He took
Mary with him as a servant for his daughters. On a
beach in Bermuda, Mary chanced to meet her
mother among a group of slaves. By this time,
Mary's mother had become mentally unbalanced
because of the cruelty of slavery, which had separated her from her children.

Mary's chores in Bermuda consisted of planting
and maintaining the garden, "all the household
work, and attending upon a horse and cow
besides,— going also upon all errands." Her owner
was an abusive person with offensive habits.

> He had an ugly fashion of stripping himself
> quite naked, and ordering me then to wash him
> in a tub of water. . . Sometimes when he called
> me to wash him I would not come, my eyes were
> so full of shame. He would them come to beat
> me. One time I had plates and knives in my
> hand, and I dropped both . . . [and] some of the
> plates were broken. He struck me so severely for
> this, that at last I defended myself, for I thought
> it was high time to do so. I then told him I would
> not live longer with him, for he was a very inde-
> cent man—very spiteful, and too indecent; with
> no shame for his servants, no shame for his own
> flesh.

Mary finally convinced Mr. D—— to sell her to a
Mr. Wood, who took her to Antigua.

Mary had saved one hundred dollars with
which to purchase her freedom; however, Mr. Wood

refused to release her. For a slave to have one hundred dollars was highly unusual, but many hardworking and thrifty slaves did manage to accumulate money. Mary Prince is a good example of a shrewd, hardworking woman who took on many extra duties to earn money with which to buy her freedom.

> I took in washing, and sold coffee and yams and other provisions to the captains of ships. I did not sit still idling during the absence of my owners; for I wanted, by all honest means, to earn money to buy my freedom. Sometimes I bought a hog cheap on board ship, and sold it for double the money on shore; and I also earned a good deal by selling coffee. By this means I by degrees acquired a little cash.

Her owner went to the country to a place called Date Hill. Here Mary Prince went to her first prayer meeting, and she was so affected by the services that she decided to become a member of the Moravian Church.* At this church she met her future husband, Daniel James. "He was a carpenter and cooper to his trade; an honest, hard-working, decent black man, and a widower." They were married Christmas 1826 in the Moravian Chapel. Law forbade their marriage in the English church because "English marriage is not allowed to slaves; and no free man can marry a slave woman."

When her owners, the Woods, found out about her marriage, they were very angry. Mrs. Wood was more disturbed by the marriage than Mr. Wood. "She said that she would not have nigger men

---

*A Protestant sect founded in Saxony by emigrants from Morovia.

about the yards and premises." Mary was very unhappy in her marriage because she was a slave and not a free woman.

When her owners traveled to England to put their son in school and bring their daughters home, Mary accompanied them. After enduring as much as she could from the Woods in England, Mary ran away to the Moravian mission, whose members welcomed her.

Although Mary was free in England, she would not be free if she were to return to the West Indies, as she learned from the legal advisers of the Anti-Slavery Society. Mr. Wood refused to free her, so Mary could not return to her husband, who had remained in Antigua.

The narrative concludes with Mary still hoping to find a way to be free in both England and the West Indies so she could return to her husband in Antigua. She ends her narrative by contradicting those whites who claim that slaves do not want to be free.

> Is it happiness for a driver in the field to take down his wife or sister or child, and strip them, and whip them in such a disgraceful manner?—women that have had children exposed in the open field to shame! There is no modesty or decency shown by the owner to his slaves; men, women, and children are exposed alike. . . . This is slavery. I tell it, to let the English people know the truth; and I hope they will never leave off to pray God, and call loud to the great King of England, till all the poor blacks be given freedom, and slavery done up for evermore.

The Beautiful Slave

Published in *The Colored American*, July 8, 1837, New York.[3]

The Colored American was a black abolitionist newspaper that often published descriptions of the horrors of slavery. The account is preceded by an introduction written by the editor of the newspaper.

A copy of the New York Sun, containing the following, has been politely forwarded to us by an unknown hand. The reader cannot fail to make many sober comments, as he [or she] peruses the interesting tale. What induced the infamous wretch to pay 4,500 dollars for a young female, at a time when slave "property" had so depreciated in value, and then to "appropriate a handsome apartment in his house to her use"? O, shame! But "many of the slaves are kindly treated." True, and when the sheriff comes, they are sold at auction. Is it right to hold a human being in constant jeopardy of receiving treatment the most cruel and vile?

THE BEAUTIFUL SLAVE

A gentleman of fortune in this city has lately received a letter from his brother who is President of one of the Mobile [Alabama] Banks, who mentions, among other matters relative to the present distressing times, some interesting incidents, touching the sale of the effects of a late merchant of that city, Mr. N——.

This gentleman was possessed of a beautiful female slave, about 18 years of age. In the North she would have been taken for a brunett [*sic*], being as unlike the French creoles as possible. Indeed, it was said that she had not a drop of French, and but precious little African blood in her veins. Nevertheless, she was a slave at the time of her master's failure, and as such became the property of his creditors. An individual (a broker) to whom Mr. N—— owed some 10,000 dollars, determined to possess himself of this girl, if possible, and it was unlike the intention of the broken merchant to redeem her at all hazards. All the creditors except the broker agreed that N—— might retain his slave on giving a good endorsed 12 months note for 1,500 dollars with interest. He alone demanded the sale of the girl under the hammer, and the unfortunate merchant was compelled to submit, determining, however, to have some of his friends buy her for him.

The day of sale having arrived, Mr. N—— was under no apprehension but that he could retain his Martha for something less than 2,000 dollars, and he had made arrangements to meet that sum in full, and commissioned one of this friends to make the purchase for him. But what was his surprise and indignation to see his refractor creditor make the first bid 2,000! He was not thus to be baulked, and under instructions, his friend bid 2,600. The creditor, however, persisted in overbidding, until the beautiful Martha was struck off to him at 4,500!

It was utterly out of the power of the broken merchant to raise money even for the last bid he had made upon his Martha, had it succeeded in purchasing her, and his creditor would doubtless have still overbid him, had he gone higher. He must therefore lose her or pay the full amount of the 10,000 dollar debt, which it was impossible for him to do. What was then to be done? Martha would never consent to part with her master. He had purchased her on his first arrival at the South, more than eight years ago, at her own request, she then living about twenty miles from Mobile. He had given her every advantage of education, and brought her up as tenderly as though she were his own daughter, and now she would sooner part with life itself than become a slave!

Her feelings on learning her situation, (for N—— had carefully concealed the announcement of the sale from her) were probably similar to those which the proud daughter of any citizen would experience in a like predicament, for the fact of her being a slave was known to but a few in Mobile. She therefore sent word to her purchaser that she would never leave her present abode alive. In answer to this message, he sent two officers to take her into custody.

Meantime, Mr N— had encouraged her that she should certainly escape her doom and embark for New York, whither he would join her in a short time, never again to return, and he would there marry her.

Martha was shortly after this placed in the

common jail at Mobile, as a stubborn servant, but fortunately the keeper interested himself in her behalf, and she enjoyed equal comforts to those of her master's house.

Just ten days after this, Martha signified her consent to leave the prison, and take up her abode with her new master, the heartless creditor of N——. With pleasure and surprise she was liberated by the purchaser, who appropriated a handsome apartment in his house for her use. The same night she started for Savannah per express, unknown to anyone save the faithful N——. A 1,000 dollar reward was immediately offered for her apprehension, and the detection of those who had aided in her escape, and on the fifth day the reward was doubled—messengers also having been sent to New Orleans, and in several other directions.

A fortnight passed, and no tidings of the beautiful slave Martha. Every one suspected, though none could prove that her former master had aided in her escape. Mr. N——had now nearly arranged his affairs, and was about to leave Mobile. His stubborn creditor had tried, by every means in his power, to procure an indictment against him, but without success. Even on the evening before N——'s departure, his friend, at his desire, called upon the creditor to endeavor if possible to purchase a release of the title to Martha.

"No," replied the broker, "I'd sooner spend 10,000 dollars than be tricked by the infernal Yankee!" N— took his leave, depositing 800 dollars with his friend, which was all the spare money he had, and instructing him to purchase with it the freedom of Martha, if possible.

Within one month from the time N—— left

Mobile, the extensive house of R. M.& Brothers, cotton brokers, stopped payment,—and in due time, the sale of their personal property devolved upon an auctioneer. Among the living chattels disposed of, the title to the beautiful slave Martha, (then absent), but who cost 4,500 dollars, was struck off to the friend of N—— for sixty-two dollars!

This narrative is not fiction—the writer of the letter first mentioned being the identical purchaser of the slave Martha. His immediate object in writing to the gentleman who furnished us with the above, was to ascertain the whereabouts of his friend N—, as he had not been able to hear from him since his important purchase, though he had immediately written to New York, acquainting N—— with it. We have been promised an introduction to the heroine of this narrative, and her now happy husband.

Eliza

From the male narrative *"Truth Is Stranger Than Fiction," An Autobiography of the Rev. Josiah Henson*, published in 1859.[4]

Eliza is the name of the slave immortalized in *Uncle Tom's Cabin* by her desperate escape across the broken ice floes of a river. Josiah Henson claimed that Stowe took her character of Eliza from an account of a true incident that was first reported in the *Reminiscences of Levi Coffin.* In his autobiography, Henson gives the truthful version of this thrilling incident, as told him by the woman herself.

> She said she was a slave from Kentucky, the property of a man who lived a few miles back from the Ohio River, below Ripley, Ohio. Her master and mistress were kind to her, and she had a comfortable home, but her master got into some pecuniary* difficulty, and she found that she and her only child were to be separated. She

*Of or pertaining to money.

had buried two children, and was doubly attached to the child, over two years old. When she found that it was to be taken from her, she was filled with grief and dismay, and resolved to make her escape that night, if possible. She watched her opportunity, and when darkness settled down, and all the family had retired to sleep, she started with her child in her arms and walked straight toward the Ohio River. She knew that it was frozen over at that season of the year, and hoped to cross without difficulty on the ice; but when she reached its banks, at daylight, she found that the ice had broken up and was slowly drifting in large cakes. She ventured to go to a house near by, where she was kindly received and permitted to remain through the day. She hoped to find some way to cross the river the next night, but there seemed little prospect of any one being able to cross in safety, for during the day the ice became more broken and dangerous to cross. In the evening she discovered that pursuers were near the house, and with desperate courage she determined to cross the river or perish in the attempt. Clasping her child in her arms, she darted out of the back door and ran toward the river, followed by her pursuers, who had just dismounted from their horses when they caught sight of her. No fear or thought of personal danger entered Eliza's mind, for she felt that she would rather be drowned than be captured and separated from her child. Clasping her babe to her bosom with her left arm, she sprang on to the first cake of ice, then from that to another and another. Sometimes the cake she was on would sink beneath her weight, then she would slide her child on to the next cake, pull herself on with her hands, and so continue the hazardous journey. She became wet to the waist with ice-water, and her hands were benumbed with cold, but as she made her way from one cake of ice to another, she felt that surely the Lord was preserving and upholding her, and that nothing could harm her.

When she reached the Ohio side, near Ripley, she was completely exhausted and almost breathless. A man who had been standing on the bank watching her progress with amazement, and expecting every moment to see her go down, assisted her up the bank. After she had recovered her strength a little, he directed her to a house on the hill in the outskirts of the town. She made her way to the place, and was kindly received and cared for. It was not considered safe for her to remain there during the night, so, after resting awhile, and being provided with food and dry clothing, she was conducted to a station on the underground railroad, a few miles farther from the river. The next night she was forwarded on from station to station to our house in Newport, where she arrived safely and remained several days.

Other fugitives arrived in the meantime, and Eliza and her child were sent with them by the Greenville branch of the underground railroad to Sandusky, Ohio. They reached that place in safety, and crossed the lake to Canada, locating finally at Chatham, Canada West.

Patsey

Included in *Twelve Years a Slave*. By Solomon Northup, published in 1853.[5]

Patsey was slim and straight. She stood erect as the human form is capable of standing. There was an air of loftiness in her movement, that neither labor, nor weariness, nor punishment could destroy. Truly, Patsey was a splendid animal, and were it not that bondage had enshrouded her intellect in utter and everlasting darkness, would have been chief among ten thousand of her people. She could leap the highest fences, and a fleet hound it was indeed, that could outstrip her in a race. No horse could fling her from his back. She was a skillful teamster.* She turned as true a furrow as the best, and at splitting rails there were none who could excel her. When the order to halt was heard at night, she would have her mules at the crib, unharnessed, fed and curried, before uncle Abram had found his hat. Not, however, for all or any of these, was she chiefly famous. Such lightning-like motion

---

*The driver of a team of horses.

was in her fingers as no other fingers ever possessed, and therefore it was, that in cotton picking time, Patsey was queen of the field.

She had a genial and pleasant temper, and was faithful and obedient. Naturally, she was a joyous creature, a laughing, light-hearted girl, rejoicing in the mere sense of existence. Yet Patsey wept oftener, and suffered more, than any of her companions. She had been literally excoriated. Her back bore the scars of a thousand stripes; not because she was of an unmindful and rebellious spirit, but because it had fallen to her lot to be the slave of a licentious master and a jealous mistress. She shrank before the lustful eye of the one, and was in danger even of her life at the hands of the other, and between the two, she was indeed accursed. In the great house, for days together, there were high and angry words, poutings and estrangement, whereof she was the innocent cause. Nothing delighted the mistress so much as to see her suffer, and more than once, when Epps [the owner] had refused to sell her, has she tempted me with bribes to put her secretly to death, and bury her body in some lonely place in the margin of the swamp. Gladly, would Patsey have appeased this unforgiving spirit, if it had been in her power, but not like Joseph dared she escape from Master Epps, leaving her garment in his hand. Patsey walked under a cloud. If she uttered a word in opposition to her master's will, the lash was resorted to at once, to bring her to subjection; if she was not watchful when about her cabin, or when walking in the yard, a billet of wood, or a broken bottle perhaps, hurled from her mistress's hand, would smite her unexpected in the face. The enslaved victim of lust and hate, Patsey had no comfort of her life.

Eliza

Twelve Years A Slave. By Solomon Northup, published in 1853.[6]

Solomon Northup had met Eliza at a New Orleans slave market. Accompanying her were her two children, Randall and Emily.

> [Eliza] was the slave of Elisha Berry, a rich man, living in the neighborhood of Washington. She was born, I think, on his plantation. Years before, he had fallen into dissipated habits, and quarreled with his wife. In fact, soon after the birth of Randall [Eliza's son] they [Elisha Berry and his wife] separated. Leaving his wife and daughter in the house they had always occupied, he erected a new one near by, on the estate. Into this house he brought Eliza, and on the condition of her living with him, she and her children were to be emancipated. She resided with him there nine years, with servants to attend upon her, and provided with every comfort and luxury of life. Emily, [her daughter,] was his child!

Finally, her young mistress, [Mrs. Berry's daughter], who had always remained with her mother at the homestead, married a Mr. Jacob Brooks. At length, for some cause, (as I gathered from her relation), beyond Berry's control, a division of his property was made. [Eliza] and her children fell to the share of Mr. Brooks. During the nine years she had lived with Berry, in consequence of the position she was compelled to occupy, she and Emily had become the object of Mrs. Berry and her daughter's hatred and dislike. Berry himself she represented as a man of naturally a kind heart, who always promised her that she should have her freedom, and who, she had no doubt, would grant it to her then, if it were only in his power. As soon as [the Brooks] thus came into the possession and control of the daughter, it became very manifest they would not live long together. The sight of Eliza seemed to be odious to Mrs. Brooks; neither could she bear to look upon the child, her half-sister, and as beautiful as she was.

The day she was led into the pen, Brooks had brought her from the estate into the city, under pretence that the time had come when her free papers were to be executed, in fulfillment of her master's promise. Elated at the prospect of immediate liberty, she decked herself and little Emmy in their best apparel, and accompanied him with a joyful heart. On their arrival in the city, instead of being baptized into the family of freemen, she was delivered to the trader Burch. The paper that was executed was a bill of sale. The hope of years was blasted in a moment. From the high of most exulting happiness to the utmost depths of wretchedness, she had that day descended. No wonder that she wept, and filled the pen with wailings and expressions of heart-rending woe .

At the sale, Randall was sold first. Emily pleaded with the buyer to buy her and her daughter also. The man said that he could not afford to buy three slaves. Freeman, the slave trader, turned round to her, savagely, with his whip in his uplifted hand, and ordered her to stop her noise, or he would flog her. It was to no avail, Randall left with his new owner. Eliza was next on the auction block. She sold for seven hundred dollars.

When Eliza heard [about] it, she was in an agony again. By this time she had become haggard and hollow-eyed with sickness and with sorrow. It would be a relief if I could consistently pass over in silence the scene that now ensued. It recalls memories more mournful and affecting than any language can portray. I have seen mothers kissing for the last time the faces of their dead offspring; I have seen them looking down into the grave, as the earth fell with a dull sound upon the coffins, hiding [loved ones] from their eyes forever; but never have I seen such an exhibition of intense, unmeasured, and unbounded grief, as when Eliza was parted from her child. She broke from her place in the line of women, and rushing down to where Emily was standing caught her in her arms. The child, sensible of some impending danger, instinctively fastened her hands around her mother's neck, and nestled her little head upon her bosom. Freeman [the slave trader] sternly ordered her to be quiet, but she did not heed him. He caught her by the arm and pulled her rudely, but she only clung the closer to the child. Then, with a volley of great oaths, he struck her such a heartless blow, that she staggered backward, and was like to fall. Oh! how piteously then did she beseech and beg and pray that they might not be separated. Why could they not be purchased together? Why not let her have one of her dear children? "Mercy, mercy, master!" she cried, falling on her knees. "Please master, buy Emily. I can never work any if she is taken from me: I will die."

Freeman interfered again, but, disregarding him, she still plead [*sic*] most earnestly, telling how Randall had been taken from her—how she never would see him again, and now it was too bad—oh, God! it was too bad, too cruel, to take her away from Emily—her pride—her only darling, that could not live, it was so young, without its mother!

Finally, after much more supplication, the purchaser of Eliza stepped forward, evidently affected, and said to Freeman he would buy Emily, and asked him what her price was.

"What is her price? Buy her?" was the responsive interrogatory of Theophilus Freeman. And instantly answering his own inquiry, he added, "I won't sell her. She's not for sale."

The man remarked he was not in need of one so young—that it would be of no profit to him, but since the mother was so fond of her, rather than see them separated, he would pay a reasonable price. But to his humane proposal Freeman was entirely deaf. He would not sell her then on any account whatever. There were heaps and piles of money to make from her, he said, when she was a few years older. There were men enough in New-Orleans who would give five thousand dollars for such an extra, handsome, fancy piece as Emily would be, rather than not get her. No, no, he would not sell her then. She was a beauty—a picture—a doll—one of the regular blood—none of your thick-lipped, bullet-headed, cotton-picking niggers—if she was might he be d—d.

When Eliza heard Freeman's determination not to part with Emily, she became absolutely frantic.

"I will not go without her. They shall not take her from me," she fairly shrieked, her shrieks commingling with the loud and angry voice of Freeman, commanding her to be silent.

Eliza never after saw or heard of Emily or Randall. Day nor night, however, were they never absent from her memory. In the cotton field, in the cabin, always and everywhere, she was talking of them—often to them, as if they were actually present. Only when absorbed in that illusion, or asleep, did she ever have a moment's comfort afterward.

Aunt Sally

Aunt Sally; Or, The Cross The Way of Freedom. A Narrative of the Slave-life and Purchase of the Mother of Rev. Isaac Williams, of Detroit, Michigan, published in 1858.[7]

Aunt Sally was born about 1796, although "a slave's precise age is a matter of conjecture . . .," near Fayetteville, North Carolina. Her slave parents were not happy when she was born; ". . .it was no joy to them to rear children for the same fate."

As a young slave, Sally attended a religious service, a camp meeting, and returned greatly disturbed.

> In distress and uncertainty Sally lay down that night to sleep, and, for the first time in her life, tried to pray. So guilty did she feel herself, that she would not have dared to do it, if that gentle invitation had not rung in her ears—
>
> *"Sinner, come to me,*
> *And thou shalt rest and glory see."*

The next day while working in the fields, she faint-
ed. Her companions picked her up and carried her
to the nearest cabin, where she lay in a coma for
two days. On the third day "this trance-like state
passed away, and she revived and was herself
again." Sally continued to work in the fields until
the old owner died and the slaves were transferred
"to the rule of young Mas'r Harry . . ."

Mr. Harry's new wife took Sally from the fields
and into the house. At this time Sally was about
thirteen years old, and the new wife, deciding it
was time for Sally to marry, chose Sally's husband-
to-be.

> What think you of a system which gives such
> unlimited control, not only over the time and
> labor of men and women, but over their most
> sacred affections? Sally had never seen him, and
> knew nothing about the matter, till one day,
> when she was in the house, her mistress said—"
> Well, Sally, you're thirteen years old, and I want
> you to be married".

Sally married a slave, Abram Williams and bore
him two sons. A third child died shortly after the
birth. "Sally did not mourn for it, she was glad it
had escaped the misery of their earthly lot."
Eventually, she had three living children.

Sally's owner hired her out, a common occur-
rence when the slaveholder needed extra money.
Sally was very happy with the arrangement.

> What was it that made her so happy? The
> privilege of working every moment for the sup-
> port of herself and her children, and of paying
> out of her earnings six dollars every month to
> her master? Verily happiness is not absolute, but
> relative, in this world.

Sally's "husband" had been sold to a plantation near Fayetteville, but came to visit Sally and the children often. "He was a kind and affectionate man, but he had a weak character. He had . . . fallen into a habit of gambling . . ." When Abram's owner discovered that he had developed a gambling habit, the owner threatened to jail him for a year. This threat so frightened Abram that he avoided the gambling room for almost a year. However, one night the old temptation returned and Abram began gambling again. The owner heard of it, and as he had threatened, threw Abram in jail and then sold him to New Orleans.

Four years after Abram had gone to Louisiana, Sally's owner decided that she needed a new husband. Sally chose for herself a free black man, Beggs, "because she thought he could never be sold away from her".

The wife of Sally's owner, who had been ailing for many years, died. Her property, including the slaves, was divided between her brothers and their children. Sally and her sons were left to a nephew, "a dissipated young man, who had wasted all his property, and had been waiting impatiently for his old aunt's death, that he might receive his portion of her estate."

This degenerate person wanted to convert his share of the inheritance into cash. Sally's three sons, Daniel, Isaac, and Lewis, were sold at a public aution in Fayetteville. Only Lewis was sold to a plantation close to her. Though Sally was married to a freeman, her children could be sold because children took the condition of the mother.

Eventually Sally was also sold (and resold). A Mrs. Cone assigned her to the kitchen.

All the cooking for the house was to be done by her, and in addition to this, she had her daily task of sewing on the shirts and trowsers for the slaves. This she often had to do a night, by the light of the fire. . . . (also) she sat up at night to knit and to do little odd jobs of sewing, that she might earn money . . . for herself.

Sally joined the Baptist Church soon after the Cones bought her, and occasionally she was allowed to attend Sunday services. Sunday afternoon was the favored time for training dogs that were used to hunt blacks. Such practices, which Sally witnessed on her way to worship, reinforced her belief in the evil of slavery.

When not in use, the dogs were always kept chained, and no colored person was allowed to speak to them, or to feed them, under the penalty of a severe whipping. At training times, the dogs were let loose, and put on the track of a little negro [sic] boy, who was made to climb a tree. When they could trace him unerringly to his place of concealment, they were considered trained.

Sally's son, Isaac, who had obtained his freedom, had become a minister of a small church, and he set about to buy his mother's freedom. Isaac wrote frequent letters to the Cones, pleading with them to sell his mother. Mr. Cone would gladly have sold her, but his wife, to whom Sally belonged, consistently refused.

To quiet her conscience, Mrs. Cone set a price of four hundred dollars for Sally's freedom. Mrs. Cone believed Isaac would be unable to raise such a large sum, but Isaac, did at last raise the sum, and a free Sally joined her son in Detroit. The narrative concludes:

Uniformly cheerful, she looks at her mercies rather than her trials. She knows not whether her first husband is living or dead. She has never heard a word from her little Lewis, since the trader told her of his having been sold. . . . When she last heard of her son Daniel, he was in jail in Virginia, having escaped from a cruel master in North Carolina, and fled toward the North, and been taken up and imprisoned as a runaway slave. . . . In every affliction she has trusted the Lord; and felt that He could turn her sorrows to blessings. Truly, to her the Cross has been the Way of Freedom.

Louisa Picquet, the Octoroon

Louisa Picquet, the Octoroon: A Tale of Southern Life by Rev. H. Mattison, published in 1861[8]

This narrative is based on an interview of Louisa Picquet by Rev. Mattison in Buffalo, New York, in May 1860.

> Louisa Picquet was born in Columbia, South Carolina.
>
> She is a little above the medium height, easy and graceful in her manners, of fair complexion and rosy cheeks with dark eyes, a flowing head of hair with no perceptible inclination to curl, and every appearance, at first view, of an accomplished white lady. No one, not apprised of the fact would suspect that she had a drop of African blood in her veins; indeed, few will believe it, at first, even when told of it.

Though it is not obvious from her physical appearance that Louisa is black, her race can be discerned through her behavior, Rev. Mattison declared. In addition to having a

. . . certain menial-like diffidence, her plantation expressions and pronunciation, her inability to read or write, together with her familiarity with and readiness in describing plantation scenes and sorrows, all attest the truthfulness of her declaration that she has been most of her life a slave. Besides, her artless simplicity and sincerity are sufficient to dissipate the last doubt.

Chapter 2 begins the life story of Louisa. Louisa's mother, Elizabeth, was a slave on the plantation of John Randolph, by whom Elizabeth had Louisa. There were laws that forbade a slave mother from revealing the father—if the father were white— under penalty of death.

[Elizabeth] was a slave owned by John Randolph,[*] and was a seamstress in his family. She was fifteen years old when I was born. Mother's mistress had a child only two weeks older than me. Mother's master, Mr. Randolph, was my father. So mother told me. She was forbid to tell who was my father, but I looked so much like Madame Randolph's baby that she got dissatisfied, and mother had to be sold. Then mother and me was sent to Georgia, and sold. I was a baby . . . about two months old, maybe older.

The family was sold in Georgia to a Mr. Cook, by whom Elizabeth had three more children. Louisa grew up in his household, but by the time she was fifteen years old, Mr. Cook, a married man who had children by Louisa's mother, also made advances toward Louisa.

---

[*]This John Randolph is not to be confused with John Randolph, the first president of the Continental Congress, 1774–75.

At breakfast-time, I had to take his breakfast up to him. . . . The door was open wide enough for a person to come in. Then he ordered me, in a sort of commanding way (I don't want to tell what he said), and told me to shut the door. At the same time he was kind of raising up out of the bed; then I began to cry; but before I had time to shut the door, a gentleman walk out of another room close by, picking his nails, and looking in the room as he passed on.

Embarrassed at almost being caught red-handed, Mr. Cook ordered Louisa to go downstairs to get him some salt. A young slave boy delivered the salt instead.

. Mr. Cook continued his pursuit of Louisa; he gave her money with which to purchase a new dress. He tried again to lure her into his bedroom, but again she refused.

Finally, to satisfy his debts, her owner sold Louisa, her mother, and her siblings. The mother and one child, a boy, were sold to Texas, and Louisa was bought by Mr. Williams, a "New Orleans gentleman."

Q.—"Had you any children while in New Orleans?"
A.—"Yes, I had four."
Q.—"Who was their father?"
A.—"Mr. Williams."
Q.—"Was it known that he was living with you?"
A.—"Every body knew I was housekeeper, but he never let on that he was the father of my children. I did all the work in his house—nobody there but me and the children. . . ."
Q.—"Were your children mulattoes?"
A.—"No, sir! They were all white. They look just like him . . ."

While in New Orleans, Louisa found God. She began to realize that her living arrangements were immoral.

> A.—". . . I wished he would sell me, or 'put me in his pocket'—that's the way we say—because I had no peace at all. I'd rather die than live in that way. Then he got awful mad, and said nothin' but death should separate us; and if I run off, he'd blow my brains out. . . . "
> Q.—"Do not the slave women usually have husbands, or those they call their husbands?"
> A.—"Yes, sir; some of them do; but some of them do not. They can't have any husbands, because their masters have them all the time."

Her owner and lover, the New Orleans gentleman Mr. Williams, was not rich. He had had to borrow the money to buy Louisa. Mr. Williams bought her to exploit her sexually. After Louisa bore him several children, Mr. Williams died. "I didn't cry nor nothin,' for I was glad he was dead; for I thought I could have some peace and happiness then. I was left free, and that made me so glad I could hardly believe it myself."

Under the conditions of Mr. Williams's will, Louisa and her children were free. She left New Orleans and settled in Cincinnati because "I had no money to go further; and I met all my friends there (Cincinnati) that I had known when I was small, in Georgia."

Three years after moving to Cincinnati, she married Henry Picquet.

> Q.—"Is he a white man or colored?"
> A.—"He's a mulatto. His mother is brown skin, and his father white, and that makes a mulatto, you know."
> Q.—"Who was his father?"

A.—"He was a Frenchman, in Georgia. He bought my husband's mother, and lived with her public. . . . She had four other children besides my husband."

Q.—"Were they slaves?"

A.—"Yes. They all belong to Mr. Picquet, but he never uses them as slaves. They are his children."

Q.—"How did they get free?"

A.—"Why, when he got married, he sent them all to Cincinnati, the mother and five children. It would be unpleasant for them all to stay there together" (i.e., his wife, and concubine and her children).

Rev. Mattison continued questioning Louisa about the life of her husband, Henry.

Q.—"Had your husband ever been married before?"

A.—"Yes, he married a slave-woman there."

Q.—. . . "Do they have a minister to marry them out on the plantations?"

A.—"No. . . . They ask the master, and then have little bit of frolic, and sometimes they don't have that."

Henry had "married" Eliza, a laundress. When her original owner died, the heirs sold her and then divided the money among themselves.

Then a gentleman in Macon bought Eliza for himself. Then Henry felt so bad about it that, pretty soon, he went to see her. He went there with the intention of buyin' her and her baby, which was Henry's. Mr. Picquet, Henry's father, was goin' to let him have the money. So, when he got there, he found it different from what he expected. He found he could not have her any more for his wife. You see, the gentleman had bought her for himself. So my husband writ to his father that he could not get his wife, but he could some day buy the child. Then his father, Mr. Picquet, sent on the money, and he bought the child, and brought it away.

While living in New Orleans with Mr. Williams, Picquet received a letter from her mother. Louisa's hopes were raised that perhaps she could buy her mother's freedom. After moving to Cincinnati, she found a Texas address for her mother and began corresponding with her. Her mother wrote that Louisa could purchase her and Louisa's younger brother for 2,500 dollars.

Louisa began private efforts to raise the money to purchase their freedom. She visited churches and organizations, soliciting money for the fund to free her mother. Louisa advertised in newspapers for assistance. She left Ohio for New York City and then went to Buffalo, where she continued her efforts to raise the needed money.

Everyone did not accept her for what she was. At one church, a Reverend Henry Slicer, a Baptist minister, "looked sternly at Mrs. Picquet, and with an imperious air said, "*You* a colored woman? You're no negro [*sic*]. Where did you come from? . . . " As he went away, he looked at Mr. Hill and said, "She's no negro," and thus ended the possibility of assistance from Rev. Henry Slicer. The minister believed that Picquet was white and that she was asking for money under false pretenses.

In October 1860 Louisa's efforts were successful and she was able to purchase her mother with 900 dollars that had been raised. Perhaps because Louisa had not obtained the entire 2,500 dollars, she could not also buy her brother's freedom. The narrative ends without telling what happened to Louisa's brother.

Harriet Jacobs (Linda Brent)

Incidents in the Life of A Slave Girl by Harriet Jacobs (Linda Brent) published in 1861.[9]

In the preface to her narrative, *Incidents in the Life of A Slave Girl*, Harriet Jacobs, using the pseudonym Linda Brent, states:

> *. . . I do earnestly desire to arouse the women of the North to a sense of the condition of millions of women in the South, still in bondage, suffering what I suffered, and far worse.*

She is publishing her narrative to expose the sexual abuses that slave women are subjected to. Maria Child, the editor of the work, writes in the Preface:

> This peculiar phase of Slavery has generally been kept veiled, but the public ought to be made acquainted with its monstrous features, and I willingly take the responsibility of presenting them with the veil withdrawn. I do this for the sake of my sisters in bondage, who are suffering wrongs so foul, that our ears are too delicate to listen to them.

Harriet Jacobs says, "I was a poor slave girl, only fifteen years old," when Dr. Flint had begun "to whisper foul words in my ear." Linda recounts that Dr. Flint, who was about fifty-five years old, wanted her to violate every moral principle that her grandmother had taught her.

> . . . he was my master. I was compelled to live under the same roof with him—where I saw a man forty years my senior daily violating the most sacred commandments of nature. He told me I was his property; that I must be subject to his will in all things.
>
> The degradation, the wrongs, the vices, that grow out of slavery, are more than I can describe. . . . She [the young slave woman] will become prematurely knowing in evil things. . . . That which commands admiration in the white woman only hastens the degradation of the female slave.

Linda could not reveal what was happening to her because Dr. Flint had warned her that he would kill her if she were not "as silent as the grave." As a result, she never told her grandmother what she was enduring.

The life of a slave girl was very different from the life of a free child. Virtue was expected in white women, while in black women it was considered incongruous and unprofitable. The fertility of slave women was to increase the owner's property, thus his wealth. Owners could not become rich if slave women were virtuous.

Finally, Linda revealed her problem to Mrs. Flint, who was of little assistance. "The mistress, who ought to protect the helpless victim, has no other feelings towards her but those of jealousy and rage."

Eventually Linda fell in love with a young carpenter, a free black man; yet, she constantly had to remember that she ". . . was a slave, and that the laws gave no sanction the marriage of such. . . " Slaves, under law, were forbidden to marry; they had "no right to any family ties of their own; . . . they were created merely to wait upon the family of the mistress." She told Dr. Flint that she wanted to "marry" this man. "How dare you tell me so!" he exclaimed. "I supposed you thought more of yourself; that you felt above the insults of such puppies."

I replied, "If he is a puppy I am a puppy, for we are both of the negro [*sic*] race. It is right and honorable for us to love each other. The man you call a puppy never insulted me, sir, and he would not love me if he did not believe me to be a virtuous woman." He sprang upon me like a tiger, and gave me a stunning blow. It was the first time he had ever struck me, and fear did not enable me to control my anger. When I had recovered a little from the effects, I exclaimed, "You have struck me for answering you honestly. How I despise you"!

Slave owners not only forced their will on enslaved women but also on enslaved men. Frequently slave men were forced to withdraw to allow white men to abuse their wives and daughters.

Some poor creatures have been so brutalized by the lash that they will sneak out of the way to give their masters free access to their wives and daughters. Do you think this proves the black man to belong to an inferior order of beings? What would you be, if you had been born and brought up a slave, with generations of slaves for ancestors? I admit that the black man is infe-

61

rior. But what is it that makes him? It is the ignorance in which white men compel him to live; it is the torturing whip that lashes manhood out of him; it is the fierce bloodhounds of the South, and the scarcely less cruel human bloodhounds of the North, who enforce the Fugitive Slave Law.* They do the work.

No pen can give an adequate description of the all-pervading corruption produced by slavery. The slave girl is reared in an atmosphere of licentiousness and fear. The lash and the foul talk of her master and his sons are her teachers. When she is fourteen or fifteen, her owner, or his sons, or the overseer, or perhaps all of them, begin to bribe her with presents. If these fail to accomplish their purpose, she is whipped or starved into submission to their will. She may have had religious principles inculcated by some pious mother or grandmother, or some good mistress; she may have a lover, whose good opinion and peace of mind are dear to her heart; or the profligate men who have power over her may be exceedingly odious to her. But resistance is hopeless.

It (slavery) makes the white fathers cruel and sensual; the sons violent and licentious; it contaminates the daughters, and makes the wives wretched. And as for the colored race, it needs an abler pen than mine to describe the extremity of their sufferings, the depth of their degradation.

---

*The Fugitive Slave Law of 1850 stated that all citizens, including those in states where slavery had been abolished, were subject to punishment if they aided slaves. Any slave captured in a free state could be returned to slavery.

Flint succeeded in squashing Linda's marriage plans. He felt that the only obstacle in his way to Linda was Mrs. Flint. However, Linda meant to take control of her own life.

> I will not try to screen myself behind the plea of compulsion from a master; for it was not so. Neither can I plead ignorance or thoughtlessness. For years my master had done his utmost to pollute my mind with foul images, and to destroy the pure principles inculcated by my grandmother. . . . The influences of slavery had had the same effect on me that they had on other young girls, they had made me prematurely knowing, concerning the evil ways of the world. I knew what I did and I did it with deliberate calculation.

Linda decided to choose her own lover, Mr. Sands, a white neighbor. "It seems less degrading to give one's self than to submit to compulsion." If she had not chosen Sands, she might have had to submit to Flint's advances. She begged the reader to understand her position.

> Pity me and pardon me, O virtuous reader! You never knew what it was like to be a slave; to be entirely unprotected by law or custom; to have the laws reduce you to the condition of chattel, entirely subjected to the will of another . . . . No one can feel it more sensible than me. The painful and humiliating memory will haunt me to my dying day. Still, in looking back, calmly, on the events of my life, I feel that the slave woman ought not to be judged by the same standard as others.

After Linda had become pregnant by Mr. Sands, she told Dr. Flint. "He intimated that if I had accepted his proposals, he, as a physician, could have saved me from exposure." Moreover, he reminded her that her child would be his property, thus increasing his wealth.

When told that her newborn was a girl, her "heart was heavier than it had ever been before. Slavery is terrible for men, but it is far more terrible for women. Superadded to the burden common to all, *they* have wrongs, and sufferings, and mortifications peculiarly their own." Linda's subsequent actions were meant to save both her children, but especially her daughter.

Mr. Sands and Linda's grandmother frequently tried to purchase the children, but Dr. Flint refused to sell them. Instead of offering Linda and her children freedom, Dr. Flint offered Linda a small cottage in which she could live with Benjamin and Ellen.

Since Linda had refused all of his offers, Flint decided to send her to the plantation where her life of comparative ease would be over. Additionally, he threatened her children. "Your boy shall be put to work, and he shall soon be sold; and your girl shall be raised for the purpose of selling well." However, Linda was adamant in her refusal to surrender to him.

I had my secret hopes, but I must fight my battle alone. I had a woman's pride, and a mother's love for my children, and I resolved that out of the darkness of this hour a brighter dawn should rise for them. My master had power and law on his side; I had a determined will. There is might in each.

When Linda found out that her children were going to be sent to the plantation to be "broken in,"* rather than have them physically abused, she left her children with their father and she ran away. Dr. Flint immediately circulated reward posters.

$300 REWARD! Ran away from the sub-scriber, an intelligent, bright, mulatto girl, named Linda, 21 years of age. Five feet four inches high. Dark eyes, and black hair inclined to curl; but it can be made straight. Has a decayed spot on a front tooth. She can read and write, and in all probability will try to get to the Free States. All persons are forbidden, under penalty of the law, to harbor or employ said slave. $150 will be given to whoever takes her in the state, and $300 if taken out of the state and delivered to me, or lodged in jail.

In a fit of fury, Dr. Flint jailed Linda's brother, aunt, and children.

While escaping through the woods to reach a boat that would take her to the North, a poisonous snake bit Linda, and her journey was cut short. To find care after the snakebite, she took refuge in the home of a white woman who was a friend of her grandmother's. Linda remained at this home while Dr. Flint continued his search.

To force Linda out of hiding, Dr. Flint sold Linda's brother and children to a slave trader. Immediately after the sale, Dr. Flint asked the trader not to sell them within state, but it was too late. Mr. Sands had already purchased them.

---

*Africans were not natural slaves; they had to be taught. They had to be carefully trained in the social etiquette of slavery.

Dr. Flint's obsession with finding Linda forced her to move from her hiding place in the home of her grandmother's friend into a crawl space in her grandmother's attic. The garret was nine feet long and seven feet wide. The highest part was three feet.

> To this hole I was conveyed as soon as I entered the house. A bed had been spread on the floor. I could sleep quite comfortably on the one side but the slope was so sudden that I could not turn on the other without hitting the roof. The rats and mice ran all over my bed; but I was weary and I slept such a sleep that the wretched may. . . .It seemed horrible to sit or lie cramped in a position all day without one gleam of light. Yet I would have chosen this, rather than my lot as a slave.

From within her small, cramped hiding place, Linda's greatest suffering was her yearning to be with her children.

> My restlessness increased. I had lived too long in bodily pain and anguish of spirit. Always I was in dread that in some accident, or some contrivance, slavery would succeed in snatching my children from me. This thought drove me nearly frantic, and I determined to steer for the North Star at all hazards.

Linda stayed in the attic for seven years. At the end of this period, in 1848, Linda was taken from her hiding place and put on a boat and on the way to Philadelphia, freedom, and reunion with her children.

Mattie Jackson

*The Story of Mattie J. Jackson; Her Parentage—
Experience of Eighteen Years in Slavery—Incidents
During the War—Her Escape From Slavery. A True
Story, written and arranged by Dr. L. S. Thompson,
(Formerly Mrs. Schuyler) as given by Mattie*, pub-
lished 1866.[10]

In the preface, Mattie Jackson states:

> The object in publishing this book is to gain
> sympathy from the earnest friends of those who
> have been bound down by a dominant race in
> circumstances over which they had no control—
> a butt of ridicule and a mark of oppression; over
> whom weary ages of degradation have passed
> .... Thus I ask you to buy my little book to aid
> me in obtaining an education, that I may be
> enabled to do some good in behalf of the eleva-
> tion of my emancipated brothers and sisters.

Her narrative begins with the story of her grandfather, a slave in New York State who was freed by
his owner and given a large sum of money. A "con
artist" suggested that the grandfather accompany
him to Missouri, a slave state, to join him in speculation for promised riches. They departed on a ship
for St. Charles, Missouri.

On the passage, my grandfather was seized with a fever, and for a while was totally unconscious. When he regained his reason he found himself, near his journey's end, divested of his free papers and all others.

As a result, her grandfather was enslaved again. He eventually married a slave woman who bore him one son, Westley Jackson, Mattie's father. At age twenty-two, Westley Jackson married a slave woman, Ellen Turner. When they had been married about three years, their owner, facing financial ruin, sold all his slaves.

Because Mattie's mother had a good reputation as a servant and cook, she was bought by Mr. Charles Canory, a resident of the area. Another local resident bought her father, thus enabling her parents to live only a few miles apart. Two years later the father was resold and separated from his family, but before he could be delivered to his new owner he escaped to a free state. Mattie's mother had played an important role in her father's escape, because she hoped that one day she and the children would follow his success and also flee.

Two years after her father's escape, Mattie's mother, "with her two children, my sister and myself, attempted to. . . escape." They had reached the free state of Illinois when the slave catchers captured them and sent them to prison in St. Louis, Missouri. After four weeks in prison, William Lewis bought them.

Mattie's mother married another slave, George Brown, with whom she had two more children. But this husband too escaped—to Canada. "Thus my poor mother was again left alone, with two more children added to her misery and sorrow, to toil on her weary pilgrimage."

During the Civil War, Mrs. Lewis's emotions rose and fell with the fortunes of the Confederate Army. Mattie Jackson, of course, wanted the Union to triumph. Because of her certainty that the North would win, Mattie was very saucy to Mrs. Lewis. However, it was Mr. Lewis who meted out most of the punishment in the house. Once he gave her a severe blow with a stick of wood and ordered her to her room. Mattie refused to go and her unwillingness angered him even more.

> [He]. . . pulled me into another room and threw me on the floor, placed his knee on my stomach, slapped me on the face and beat me with his fist, and would have punished me more had not my mother interfered.

Even though Mattie was giving Mr. Lewis a good fight, tit for tat, he was getting the upper hand when Mattie's mother arrived. "He was aware my mother could usually defend herself against one man, and both of us would overpower him. . ."

Afraid of future punishments, Mattie left and went over to the Union side. She remained with the Union Army for three weeks before Mr. Lewis, asked her to return. He told her that he would take her home and no longer punish her. Instead he took her to the slave trader's compound, where she found her mother waiting for her. Lewis had put Mattie's mother there to keep her and her children from escaping. When he had Mattie in the compound, he took the mother home. Mattie remained with the slave trader for three months. While she was in the compound, she met the Union general who had helped her and informed him that Mr. Lewis had disobeyed his orders not to sell his slaves. The general immediately arrested Mr. Lewis and he was given one hundred lashes with a cowhide.

After seven months of excessive kindness, Mr. Lewis again put Mattie in the slave trader's compound—for which he received the same punishment, one hundred lashes. This time, her mother decided to take the children and escape, but they were betrayed. Again, Mr. Lewis tried to sell them, although slave speculation was then forbidden in St. Louis.

Captain Tirrell, a slave trader, was to take the family to Memphis for resale. Instead, he took them to his home until the time was better for slave sales. "His intention was to smuggle us away before the State became free." Since slave trading was illegal in St. Louis, Captain Tirrell had to be very careful in order to realize a profit on the family. He finally managed to smuggle them to Kentucky, where they were sold to different owners for extravagant prices. "My sister, aged sixteen, was sold for eight hundred and fifty dollars; I was sold for nine hundred dollars. This was in 1863."

Mattie decided that after all her years in slavery she would escape. Her plan was ingenious.

> Extensive hoops were then worn, and as I had attached my whole wardrobe under mine by a cord around my waist, it required considerable dexterity and no small amount of maneuvering to hide the fact from my mistress.

Mattie was finally able to leave her owner's home to meet the two abolitionists who were to take her to the ferry. While going up the stairs at the ferry, the cord holding her belongings broke and her clothing puddled around her feet. The incident with the clothing did not fluster Mattie. She simply stepped over them and continued up the steps.

She finally made it to freedom—Indianapolis. In the North her old yearning for literacy arose, and she began to learn to read and to write. In Indianapolis, Mattie viewed the body of the assassinated President Lincoln. "I could not be convinced of his death until I gazed upon his remains. . . " Three weeks after Mattie viewed Lincoln's body, her sister also escaped. Within three months her mother had escaped to Indianapolis. Only on her mother's seventh attempt had she finally succeeded.

Before they had been kidnapped, by Mr. Lewis, her mother had been engaged to marry a Mr. Adams. Two years and four months later they returned to St. Louis, where her mother was married within a week. Eventually, Mattie's stepfather found her and helped her and her brother come to Lawrence, Massachusetts, to live with him and his new wife. There, she says, she finally knew what freedom was because she could go to school.

In the summary of her narrative, Mattie J. Jackson relates that when she returned to St. Louis, she met her old owner Mr. Lewis. "He was so surprised that before he was aware of it he dropped a bow." With slavery abolished, Mr. Lewis and his wife had to take care of their own needs. They had to dress themselves and "brush their own flies." Mr. Lewis and his family members had lost their wealth and status in the community. Mattie ends her narrative with an essay on Christianity, which had sustained her throughout her long ordeal.

Elizabeth Keckley

Excerpts here are culled from *Behind the Scenes. Or, Thirty Years a Slave and Four Years in the White House,* by Elizabeth Keckley, published 1868.[11]

This narrative is important for scholars of Abraham Lincoln, especially those who are interested in his wife, Mary Todd Lincoln. *Behind the Scenes* is a chronological account of Keckley's life.

Keckley writes in the preface that "much has been omitted, but nothing has been exaggerated . . . . If I have portrayed the dark side of slavery, I also have painted the bright side. . . . Notwithstanding all the wrongs that slavery heaped upon me, I can bless it for one thing—youth's important lesson of self-reliance."

Keckley was born in Dinwidde (Court-House), Virginia. Both her parents were slaves. The wife of her owner, Colonel A. Burwell, gave birth to a daughter, and

> To take care of this baby was my first duty. True, I was but a child myself—only four years old—but then I had been raised in a hardy school—had been taught to rely upon myself,

and to prepare myself to render assistance to others.

Once while she was taking care of the baby, she began to rock the cradle very energetically

. . . when lo! out pitched the little pet on the floor. I instantly cried out, "Oh! the baby is on the floor"; and, not knowing what to do, I seized the fire-shovel in my perplexity, and was trying to shovel up my tender charge, when my mistress called to me to let the child alone, and then ordered that I be taken out and lashed for my carelessness. The blows were not administered with a light hand, I assure you, and doubtless the severity of the lashing has made me remember the incident so well.

Her parents lived on different plantations and they very seldom saw each other. Eventually, her father's owner sold him away which greatly saddened her mother.

My old mistress said to [the mother]: "Stop your nonsense; there is no necessity for you putting on airs. Your husband is not the only slave that has been sold from his family, and you are not the only one that has had to part.

Her parents never saw each other again, although they were able to communicate with each other for years.

One of the cruelest practices of slavery is described by Keckley:

When I was about seven years old I witnessed for the first time, the sale of a human being. . . . He [the slave] came in with a bright face, was placed in the scales, and was sold, like the hogs, at so much per pound.

The slave's mother did not know that her child was being sold. Colonel Burwell, the owner, had told her that her son would return in the morning. Day after day the mother waited for her child to return, but he never did.

> One day she was whipped for grieving for her lost boy. Colonel Burwell never liked to see one of his slaves wear a sorrowful face, and those who offended in this particular way were always punished.

Keckley continues,

> I was regarded as fair-looking for one of my race, and for four years a white man—I spare the world his name—had base designs upon me. . . . Suffice it to say, that he persecuted me for four years, and I—I—became a mother.

Eventually, a Mr. Garland bought them and he, his family, and their slaves moved to St. Louis. As he needed money, he proposed selling Keckley's mother. But Keckley "would rather work my fingers to the bone. . . even beg from street to street" before seeing her mother sold. She received permission from Mr. Garland to work outside the home to support the family, both black and white.

> I was fortunate in obtaining work, and in a short time I had acquired something of a reputation as a seamstress and dress-maker. . . . With my needle I kept bread in the mouths of seventeen persons for two years and five months.

With the constant hard work, her health began to fail.

In time, she again met Mr. Keckley, whom she had first met in Virginia. He proposed marriage, but she refused

> . . . for I could not bear the thought of bringing [more] children into slavery—of adding one single recruit to the millions bound to hopeless servitude, fettered and shackled with chains stronger and heavier than manacles of iron.

Because she did not want the child she already had to grow up in slavery, she proposed to her owner that she purchase her son's freedom and her own.

> Why should my son be held in slavery?. . . He came into the world through no will of mine, and yet, God only knows how I loved him. The Anglo-Saxon blood as well as the African flowed in his veins; the two currents commingled—one singing of freedom, the other silent and sullen with generations of despair. Why should not the Anglo-Saxon triumph—why should it be weighed down with the rich blood typical of the tropics?

At first her owner refused, but then he relented and allowed her to buy the freedom of herself and her child for twelve hundred dollars.

Knowing that she would soon be free, she consented to marry Mr. Keckley. Elizabeth began to work even harder to earn the money for her freedom. In the meantime her owner died. One of his relatives, who had come to St. Louis to settle the estate, informed Keckley that he would abide by the agreement. Like Louisa Picquet, she made up her mind to go to New York to appeal for funds with which to buy her freedom. This trip would be allowed only if she could find six people who would guarantee her return. However, before she could leave, one of her white customers, Mrs. Le Bourgois, decided that Keckley should not go to New York to "*beg* for what we should *give* you". Mrs. Le Bourgois said that she would raise the twelve hundred from among her friends and began the fund by donating two hundred dollars herself. Very soon Mrs. Le Bourgois and her friends had raised the sum and Keckley and her son were free.

Keckley very quickly repaid the loan. But now that she had purchased her freedom and repaid the loan, she was having husband trouble.

> All this time my husband was a source of trouble to me, and a burden. I determined to make a change. I had a conversation with Mr. Keckley; informed him that since he persisted in dissipation we must separate; that I was going North, and that I should never live with him again, at least until I had good evidence of his reform.

To escape from Mr. Keckley, Elizabeth moved North. She left St. Louis in the spring of 1860 and went to Baltimore, where she stayed for six months.

Keckley was not as successful in Baltimore as she had hoped and so she moved to Washington, D.C. In the nation's capital she immediately found a job paying two dollars and fifty cents per day.

Elizabeth eventually worked for Mrs. Jefferson Davis, wife of then-Senator Jefferson Davis and future president of the Confederacy, who "always appeared to me as a thoughtful, considerate man in the domestic circle." In the Davis household, impending war was openly discussed. Mrs. Davis was so sure there would be war that she suggested Keckley accompany her to the South.

> You had better go South with me; I will take good care of you. Besides, when the war breaks out, the colored people will suffer in the North. The Northern people will look upon them as the cause of the war, and I fear, in their exasperation, will be inclined to treat you harshly.

Mrs. Davis assumed that blacks would be blamed as the cause of the Civil War. But Keckley preferred "to cast my lot among the people of the North."

Because of her skill as a seamstress, Keckley began to receive commissions from some of the more important members of Washington society. The wife of General McLean wanted Keckley to work for her, but Keckley refused, saying she was unable to take on new customers. Mrs. McLean reminded Keckley, "I have often heard you say that you would like to work for the ladies of the White House. Well, I have it in my power to obtain you this privilege." Mrs. McLean was true to her word. She recommended Keckley to Mary Todd Lincoln, the wife of Abraham Lincoln, and Mrs. Lincoln sent a message asking Keckley to call at the White House.

To Keckley, Mrs. Lincoln was a lady "inclined to stoutness, about forty years of age. . . ."

> I had heard so much, in current and malicious report, of her low life, of her ignorance and vulgarity. . . . Report, I soon saw, was wrong. . . . She was confident and self-possessed, and confidence always gives grace."

Keckley soon became Mrs. Lincoln's regular dressmaker, "making fifteen or sixteen dresses for her during the spring and early part of the summer . . . . "

In the remainder of her narrative, Keckley discusses her relationship with the Lincolns. Among the revelations of her stay at the White House was the emotional devastation caused by the death of Willie, Lincoln's son.

Mrs. Lincoln is described as interfering with affairs of state, although she is "shrewd and far-seeing, and had no patience with the frank, confiding nature of the President." Mrs. Lincoln was especially critical of Lincoln's associates. In her opinion, Andrew Johnson, Lincoln's vice-president, was a demagogue; General Ulysses S. Grant was an obstinate butcher; and William Seward, the secretary of state, was unprincipled. Despite her criticism of Lincoln's colleagues, he made his own decisions. Keckley's relationship with Mrs. Lincoln continued after the president's assassination.

Keckley concludes her memoir:

> I have experienced many ups and downs, but still am stout of heart. The labor of a lifetime has brought me nothing in a pecuniary way. I have worked hard, but fortune, fickle dame, has not smiled upon me. If poverty did not weight me down as it does, I would not be toiling by day with my needle and writing by night. . . . Though poor in worldly goods, I am rich in friendships, and friends are a recompense for all the woes of the darkest pages of life. For sweet friendship's sake, I can bear more burdens than I have borne.

Harriet Tubman

Harriet, The Moses of Her People. As told to Sarah Bradford, published 1886.[12]

The narrative opens with a description of Harriet Tubman as a young slave.

> [Harriet Tubman was]. . . a little girl of perhaps thirteen years of age, darker than any of the others, and with a more decided woolliness in the hair. . . . Her only garment was a short woolen skirt, which was tied around her waist, and reached about to her knees. She seemed a dazed and stupid child and as her head hung upon her breast, she looked up with dull bloodshot eyes. . . . Bye and bye the eyes closed, and. . . she slept .

This child would become "the Moses of her People"—the woman who was a spy for the Union Army, a nurse, and the protector and liberator of many slaves,

Harriet's first owner had caused her deceptively dull appearance. When she was about thirteen years old, her owner "in an ungovernable fit of rage threw a heavy weight at the unoffending child, breaking in her skull, and causing a pressure upon her brain. . . ."

Harriet Tubman, whose name was Araminta Ross, was born in 1820 or 1821 on the eastern shore of Maryland. She was "the granddaughter of a slave imported from Africa, and has not a drop of white blood in her veins." Her parents, Benjamin Ross and Harriet Green, were slaves who managed to stay together despite the hardship of bondage. Harriet had ten brothers and sisters, three of whom she eventually rescued from slavery.

Around 1844, she married a free black man, John Tubman, but they had no children.

Harriet had been exposed to the horrors of slavery at an early age. She had heard the screams of women being flogged, seen her two older sisters taken away in a chain gang, and witnessed the grief of her parents as one by one the owner sold their children away.

As the owner's fortunes were declining, he sold slaves or hired them out to make money. "No information [was] given; they simply disappeared." One day a woman came looking for a girl to take care of a baby, and since she wanted to pay the lowest wages, "the most stupid and incapacitated of the children on the plantation was chosen to go with her," and that person was deemed to be Harriet. "It [the woman's home] was not a very fine house, but Harriet had never before been in any dwelling better than the cabins of the negro [sic] quarter." This woman was very stingy and very hard to please. She beat Harriet because Harriet did not know how to dust. Harriet, malnourished and maltreated, was finally returned to her original owner as worthless.

Again, Harriet's owner hired her out "to a man whose tyranny was worse, if possible, than that of the woman she had left." This new owner expected Harriet to do the work of a horse or a mule. ". . . the lifting of barrels of flour and other heavy weights were given to her; and powerful men often stood astonished to see this woman perform feats of strength from which they shrunk incapable." This cruelly difficult work prepared Harriet for what she would face in the future.

> Harriet still suffered from her head injury, and at times she could not work. The sting of the lash had no power to rouse her now, and the new master finding her a dead weight on his hands, returned the useless piece of property to him who was called her "owner." And while she lay there helpless, this man was bringing other men to look at her and offering her for sale at the lowest possible price; at the same time setting forth her capabilities, if once she were strong and well again.

When Harriet was in her early twenties, a rumor circulated through the slave quarters that the owner was going to sell Harriet and her brothers. Harriet and her brothers together decided to escape to the North. First they had to give their friends some hint of their plans.

> Slaves must not be seen talking together, and so it came about that their communication was often made by singing, and the words of their familiar hymns, telling of the heavenly

journey, and the land of Canaan, while they did not attract the attention of the masters, conveyed to their brethren and sisters in bondage something more than met the ear.

The slaves sang in code. Harriet strolled through the slave quarters singing:

> *When dat ar ole chariot comes,*
> *I'm gwine to lebe you,*
> *I'm boun' for de promised land,*
> *Frien's, I'm gwine to lebe you.*

After they fled the plantation, her brothers proved not to be as brave as she. The fear of the unknown was worse than their fear of slavery. They broke away and returned to the plantation. ". . . They hastened back to the known horrors of slavery, from the dread of that which was worse."

Harriet continued alone with her eyes fixed on the North Star.

> I had reasoned dis out in my mind; there was one of two things I had a right to, liberty, or death; if I could not have one, I would de oder; for no man should take me alive; I should fight for my liberty as long as my strength lasted, and when de time came for me to go, de Lord would let dem take me.

Following the North Star, Harriet walked by night and hid by day, always aware that the slave catchers were on her trail. She finally reached Philadelphia and began her involvement in the abolitionist movement. She resolved that she would rescue other enslaved Africans.

In the years that followed, all of Harriet's

wages were put aside for one purpose: to free slaves. When she had saved enough money,

> . . . she disappeared from her Northern home, and as suddenly and mysteriously she appeared some dark night, at the door of one of the cabins on a plantation, where a trembling band of fugitives, forewarned as to time and place, were [sic] anxiously awaiting their deliverer.

Once Harriet reached her destination in the South, she would walk through the woods singing the song that was "forbidden to her people at the South, but which she and her followers delight[ed] to sing together":

> *Oh go down, Moses,*
> *Way down into Egypt's land,*
> *Tell old Pharaoh,*
> *Let my people go.*

Harriet and her band of fugitive slaves followed the North Star, traveling by night and hiding by day. "She [would] carry the babies, drugged with paregoric, in a basket on her arm."

Often it was the men who could not keep up with her. They would fall to the ground or they would try to return to their old plantations. "Then the revolver carried by this bold and daring pioneer, would come out, and while pointing it at their heads she would say, 'Dead niggers tell no tales; you go on or die!'" In this way she forced them to accompany her to freedom.

She made these trips nineteen times and "brought out," i.e., brought to the free North, more than three hundred enslaved men, women, and children. Although slaveholders offered a reward of forty thousand dollars for Harriet's head, she could not be discouraged from making her trips south. She would lead her band to the "land of Canaan, the State of New York."

In 1850 Congress passed the Fugitive Slave Act. "After that," said Harriet, "I wouldn't trust Uncle Sam wid my people no longer, but I brought 'em all clar off to Canada." Harriet brought out her brother William Henry and his fiancée Catherine. As part of the escape plan, William Henry went to a tailor shop and bought a suit of clothes for a small man. He concealed the clothes in the garden of Catherine's owner—and, at a specified time, Catherine went to the garden, picked up the bundle and put on the suit. Catherine was soon missed, and the other slaves were sent to look for her.

> Presently they saw coming up from the river a well-dressed little darkey boy, and they all ceased looking for Catherine, and stared at him. He walked directly by them, round the house, and out of the gate, without the slightest suspicion being excited as to who he was. In a few weeks from that time, this party were all safe in Canada.

Following the firing on Fort Sumter, Harriet joined the conflict, even though she would never receive pay or a pension. The Union Army called her to Hilton Head to nurse Union soldiers who were dying from dysentery.* "Harriet had acquired quite a reputation for her skill in curing this disease, by a medicine which she prepared from roots which

---

*A disease with inflammation of the intestines, causing severe diarrhea.

grew near the waters which gave the disease." She also nursed victims of smallpox and other diseases.

When the Union Army went into some parts of the South, the officers discovered that the blacks were as afraid of the Yankees as they were of their owners, making it impossible for the Union officers to gain their confidence and obtain needed information. The army turned to Harriet, and she agreed to accompany the northern military expeditions for the purpose of obtaining information from the slaves remaining on the plantations.

Harriet Tubman's narrative recorded by Sarah Bradford ends with an emphasis on Christianity, which was so much a part of her life. "And as she stands in her modest way just within the celestial gate, I seem to see a kind hand laid upon her dark head, and to hear a gentle voice saying in her ear, 'Friend, come up higher!'"

Bethany Viney

The Narrative of Bethany Viney, A Slave Woman.
Published in 1890.[13]

**"*I* have but little recollection of my very early life.
My mother and her five children were owned by one
James Fletcher, Pass Run, town of Luray, Page
County, Virginia. Of my father I know nothing."**

When Bethany was nine years old, her mother
died, and soon after this, her owner, James
Fletcher, died. As was customary upon the death of
an owner, an inventory was taken of his property,
"all of which nearly was in slaves." The owner's old-
est daughter, Lucy Fletcher, inherited Bethany and
her sister, Matilda.

Bethany was hired out to a neighbor woman
who gave her food and clothes for whatever work
she could do. "She was kind to me, as I then count-
ed kindness, never whipping or starving me; but it
was not what a free-born white child would have
found comforting or needful."

When she grew up, Bethany and a slave named
Jerry wanted to marry, but Bethany refused to
marry until there was someone who could officially

marry them. One day an itinerant peddler passed by and declared that he was a minister who could marry them. He asked a few questions, which they answered satisfactorily, and then declared them husband and wife.

> I did not want him to make us promise that we would always be true to each other, forsaking all others, as the white people do in their marriage service, because I knew that at any time our masters could compel us to break such a promise...

Under the circumstances, they were as happy as they could be, especially after the birth of their daughter.

When they learned that Jerry was to be taken to Missouri, Bethany helped him to escape. Jerry's owner, Mr. White, came searching for him and asked Bethany for Jerry's whereabouts. "I then told him that Jerry had said he was willing to work, and would go to his mother's (Mr. White's mother) and serve her, but *never*, if he could help it would he be carried South."

After hiding for several weeks, Jerry returned to Bethany. They spent the night together and the next day, Sunday, they went for a walk after dinner. As they returned to the cabin, the slavetrader McCoy rode up and called to Jerry to come over to the fence.

> The excitement of the last days—the fasting and the fear—had completely cowed and broken whatever of manhood, or even of brute courage, a slave might by any possibility be presumed at any time to be possessed of, and the last remains of these qualities in poor Jerry were gone.

Jerry meekly obeyed and mounted the horse behind McCoy. McCoy then turned to Bethany, ordering her to bring Jerry's clothing.

> "Never," I screamed back to him, "never, not to save your miserable life." But Jerry said: "O Betty, 'tis no use. We can't help it." I knew this was so. I stifled my anger and my grief, brought his little bundle, into which I tucked a testament and catechism someone had given me, and shook hands "good-by" with him. So, we parted forever, in this world.

Some time later, David McCoy bought Bethany in order to sell her at the slave auction in Richmond, Virginia, and make a good profit. "I did not think so; and I determined, if possible, to disappoint him." Although she was being sold away from her child, no one would help her. Bethany was placed upon the auction block in Richmond.

> "I had been told by an old negro woman certain tricks that I could resort to, when placed upon the stand, that would be likely to hinder my sale; and when the doctor who was employed to examine the slaves on such occasions, told me to let him see my tongue, he found it coated and feverish, and turning from me with a shiver of disgust, said he was obliged to admit that at that moment I was in a very bilious condition . . . . when the auctioneer raised his hammer, and cried, "How much do I hear for this woman?" the bids were so low I was ordered down from the stand, and Eliza [another slave woman] was called up in my place. Poor thing? there were many eager bids for her; for such as she, the demands of slavery were insatiable.

As there were no buyers for Bethany, McCoy decided to keep her for himself; affecting his decision was the fact that his wife had taken a fancy to her. The McCoy household did not have enough work for Bethany, so she hired out in the neighborhood. "After a while, McCoy agreed that, if I should bring him one dollar and a half every Saturday night, he would be satisfied, and I could do what I pleased with myself." Bethany found many small jobs in the area that pleased her because she was near her child. Because of McCoy's growing confidence in her, he allowed her to have a permanent pass and to live on her own in a small cabin.

But McCoy, her owner, was deeply in debt and had to sell his property to satisfy his obligations. Bethany refused to be sold. Because of her adamancy, she asked Mr. G. J. Adams from Providence, Rhode Island, to buy her.

> Received of G. J. Adams seven hundred and seventy-five dollars ($775), it being the purchase of my negro woman Berthena, and her child Joe. The right and title to the said negro woman I warrant and defend against any person or persons whatsoever.
>
> Given under my hand and seal the 27th day of December, 1858.
> [SEAL].   DAVID MCCOY
> *BENJ. F. GRAYSON*

Before their plans were completed, however,

> ... then followed the War of the Rebellion; and it was not till a much later date, and in a different way from what I had anticipated when I left, that I saw again the old fields where I had toiled and suffered, and grasped again the hands that

before had beaten and bruised me. Eventually, after the Civil War, she moved north, to Providence, Rhode Island. She had been in Providence only three months when her son became ill and died.

Bethany, as was her habit, worked hard and saved her money. Finally, she decided to journey south. She discovered that her daughter, Charlotte, had married and was the mother of a child. After a visit of six or seven weeks, Bethany returned north, bringing her daughter, her son-in-law and her grandchild with her. Three times after her first trip she returned to the South, each time bringing relatives back with her.

At the time of the writing of her narrative, she was seventy-four years old.

> I am now, at seventy-four years of age, the owner and occupant of a small house at 21 Tufts Street, Worcester, Mass. My daughter and family are near me, in an adjoining house, also owned by me. I have three grandchildren living.
>
> My back is not so straight nor so strong, my sight is not so clear, nor my limbs so nimble as they once were; but I am still ready and glad to do whatsoever my hand findeth to do, waiting only for the call to "come up higher."
>
> Bethany Viney.
> Worcester, Mass., 1889

CHAPTER FOURTEEN

The Oral Slave Narratives

In the 1930s at the height of the Great Depression, the federal government, trying to provide employment for more than six thousand writers, created a program through which the narratives of former slaves would be collected. The ex-slaves were dying out and the government program provided a timely opportunity to record their memories. The narratives were formed from the responses of the ex-slaves to a predetermined set of questions.[14]

1. ANNA MARIA COFFEE

Anna Maria Coffee was about eighty-nine years old when her story was taken.

> I was born in North Carolina, near Ensfiel. I was a pretty big girl when the war started. But I don't know my real age, because every time I was sold they made my age just what they wanted it. I judge though I must have been about twelve or fourteen years old when the war started.

I remember hearing the big guns first fired over Fort Sumter in South Carolina. That was the starting of the war.

I was sold on the block more than once, and I was owned by eleven different owners. I was sold from my mother and father when I was just such a little tot that I can't hardly remember them at all. My father was James Arbor, and my mother, she was Abbie Freeman.

I remember being sold to old Jordan White, David Gregory, and David Gregory, Jr., John Freeman, David Teller, Bradley Pickford, Ned Pickford, Kinglin' Powells and Thomas Hurt, was my last owner.

Ned Pickford stole me from Bradley Pickford, and sold me to Kinglin' Powells, down in Warsaw, South Carolina. Kinglin' Powells took me and fourteen other slaves to Richmond, Virginia. Us left Warsaw one night on the train, and when morning come us was crossing the James River, going on to Richmond. That old James River was sure muddy that morning. They took us to the Trader Jail, and give us something to eat, and a change of clothes.

That Trader Jail was sure a big place. Us set round all day, and when night come was put in rooms up stairs, the womans and girls all on one side, and the men and boys on the other side along a narrow hall. Them sure was sad times. All us knowed it was going to be the last time us folks would be together, and most likely, none of us never see our folks no more. Every once in a while, a keeper comes through to keep them from talking and planning.

Sale day come. The market place was about a city block big, with seats fixed round like a race track. All the boys and men was fixed on one side; the big one first, and so on, down to the little ones. The womans and girls they was fixed the same way on the other side of the market.

I was put on the block and sold for 900 dollars to Thomas Hurt. He bought three brothers together, so they wouldn't be separated, and he paid 1,500 dollars for the three. I thought Marse Hurts was going to be a poor white trash owner, because he was dressed in coarse jeans pants and an old common shirt, with a big wide belt, and wore high top boots. Most all rich folks coming to sales done wore pleated bosom shirts and broadcloth suits. But when Marse Hurts open his belt he got just plenty money.

Us went to Halifax, North Carolina, and I was put to tending the children. They was just us four slaves, what he'd bought at the market in Richmond. But he had plenty of poor white trash help, what worked foe flour, meal, syrup, and for anything else he'd give them as pay for they work.

Marse Thomas and Miss Patsy didn't allow us to call the children nothing but they first name, and they had a mighty big family, fifteen of them. Miss Patsy, she was a pretty, fair, brown skin colored woman; but Marse Thomas he had take her and was the same as his wife, and they had all them children.

The children passed as white, and went to white schools and churches. Miss Patsy was good to all the slaves, and she was abolitionist at heart, but she didn't let Marse know it.

I never visited no place 'cept with the slaves at Marse Thomas's son-in-law, Ishum Hubbard's. He was abolitionist, too.

The plantation was big. I never was over all of it. Old Marse tended lots of cattle and different stock, and he raised wheat, and I just don't know what all. Miss Patsy done the cooking. . . . All us ate the same, and had plenty of it.

On such days like Sundays and holidays us didn't do no work 'cept just what had to be done. Miss Patsy, she had funny ideas about using the milk on Sunday, and she always had it poured out somewhere. But that poor white help most always took it home with them, if they could get hold of it.

Miss Patsy had lots of funny superstitions. If she heard a dog howling at night, she thought somebody was going to die in the family. And hoot owls in the house meant that somebody in the house was going to die before long; and if a black cat done cross your path it would sure bring bad luck. Then, too, if you spill salt there was sure to be some fussing.

If I was sent on an errand, and they feared I'd stayed too long, they'd say, if you stay too late the Raw Head and Bloody Bones will get you, so course they scared me, and I just tried to be back when I was supposed to be. There was an old woman living way back in the woods and folks done say that she was a witch.

One day the other slaves of Marse Thomas was all run off, and I wondered what for, none of the folks told me. So one day I goes over to Isham Hubbard's and he say: "Anna, ain't Marse Thomas done told you that you is free?" I told him, "No he didn't told me nothing but all the others is done gone." So he says for me to tell Marse Thomas that he was working me without pay, and that I was free; and if he didn't pay me something I was goin'.

I went home and told Marse Thomas what Ishum Hubbard done told me and he says:

"Anna, if you want to stay on here you can, but I
ain't going to pay you nothin'".

When Miss Patsy got a chance she talked to
me and say she didn't tell me before about being
free because Marse Thomas dared her not to; but
for me to up to Monticello, Kentucky, and she
would give me some money and my clothes. I
went and made the trip alright. I got work with
a white lawyer name Christie, and he paid me
fifty cents a week.

I went to church in Monticello, and there I
met and finally married Henry Coffee. Henry,
he'd been in the war, and belonged to the Sixth
Kentucky Cavalry. Us was the third colored
couple to get a marriage license in 1868 in
Monticello.

Then us moved to London, and Henry
farmed and done first one thing and another to
make a living. We bought a nice little place and
lived real nice, and worked in the church. What
good meetings they used to have. They sung all
the good old time songs like, "Want to go to heav-
en when I die"; "Was I born to die and lay this
body down"; and more'n I can't mention. Folks
done a lots of dancin' then, and they would
dance. . . but most generally used the fiddle.

When my daughter was big enough to go to
school, I wanted to learn, and I went to school
too. I can read and do my own writing, but lately I'se so nervous that my hand shakes so I
don't do no writin' no more. But I read most
anything.

I guess folks always will praise Lincoln,
because he was a great man, but I never heard
of him before I went to Monticello. Then I heard
what he done to free the slaves, but I know they
had to fight for what they got. I always felt

proud of Booker T. Washington, and hated to think of him havin' to die.

I lived here in Springfield [Ohio] since 1915, and I belong to the North Street Church. I got one daughter, Marthe Faghan, and there is now five generations of us livin' right here in Springfield.

2. KATE DUDLEY BAUMONT

The age of Kate Dudley Baumont was unknown at the time she dictated her narrative.

I was very young when freedom come; still I can remember lots of things, and then, too, my family been in slavery such a long time, that they often talked, and told us so much about things that happened.

I was born in Bass County, Kentucky, just twelve miles from Mt. Sterling. Father and mother were owned by a Mr. Preston of Lexington. They had been give to him when he got married—in fact, his folks give him twenty of us slaves. Mr. Preston live in Lexington, and had a fine place and several house servants. Then too, he had the farm near Mt. Sterling of about 200 acres, and twenty of us—or thereabouts— lived on that place. There was five of us children: Will, Lewis, Lucindie, Harriet and me.

Our mother died when we were very young, and our grandmother looked after us. Grandmother and my Aunt Nancy were very fine seamstresses, and they would go in town to the Preston home, and sew for weeks at a time makin' clothes for the whole family. Us children's clothes was well made and we had much more than some slaves, cause my grandmother and aunt see to it that we had things, and they made some of the things they made for the Preston girls. We did have to go bare-foot in summer time, but when the weather got cool we begun to wear shoes.

Mr. Preston would come out once in a while, and I remember him givin' us all nickel[s], and some of us older ones a. . . little bit of money.

We had a church about three miles from us and a preacher called Uncle Willis, who later was a school teacher. . .

A lot of men from our place went to war. I had two uncles what went. It was nothin' to see soldiers in our neighborhood. When the war was over, Mr. Preston give all his slaves deeds for so much land, and built them each a little four-room cottage. Some of them folks is still on that piece of land.

We moved to Lexington after a few years, and later to Georgetown. I married Mr. Robert Baumont, from Orange County, Virginia, and we went to Cincinnati. We moved from Cincinnati to Springfield about twenty-five years ago.

When we lived on the Preston farm somethin' happened that raised a lot of talk. One of the Preston girls fell in love with the Negro coachman and run off and married him in Canada. Said she never wanted to marry a white man. She never did have no white beaux as a girl.

Her father was so hurt and he said he was going to disown her, but he did give them 10,000 dollars. Then he said he never wanted them to come back to visit him or his folks, but his folks could go up to Canada and visit with her and her family.

Before, the Prestons threatened to kill the

man, but the girl she said if they killed him she would kill some of them and herself, too. She told them that she persuaded him to take her, and that she had been in love with him for years, and had tried ever so long to get him to run off with her and marry her. Old Miss like to a died, but she got over it, an took trips to Canada when she wanted to see her daughter. But the girl and her husband they never come back to her old home.

They had a family, so we heard, and he was goin' well, and had some kind of business, and later, it was said, he made a lot of money. He was a nice lookin' man, dark, but fine featured.

Preston's slaves was same as free in them times. The ones on his farm, they tended they own land and was they own boss. Folks said he let his darkies be free, and some of them talked a lot and said that when his daughter married.

I know they didn't call a doctor for every little thing in the old days, like they do now; they used home remedies, and I learned to be a midwife and nurse when I grew up. I can't think of some of the things used in them days. I know we used ground ivy for measles, and watermelon seed tea to make you babies [*sic*] kidneys act. Cucumber rinds was always good to rub on the face to remove freckles, and some people do that now.

When we went to church we sung lots of them good old hymns, like; "I want Jesus to Walk with Me; Every Day in every Hour"; Take my Burdens to the Lord"; and "Bells Done Rung and I'm Goin' Home."

Me and my two daughters is all they is left. I go up to the Pentecostal Church, on South Yellow Springs Street, and both my girls go to the Second Baptist Church.

3. AUNT MARTHA

Aunt Martha as she is known to all her "white folks," claims to be 100 years old. She was a slave to Dr. Lucas of Mt. Meigs neighborhood long before the War between the States. Dr. Lucas is one of the well known Lucas family, with whom General LaFayette spent some time while touring the United States in 1824.

Our Marster was sure good to all his "niggers." Us always had plenty to eat and plenty to wear, but the days now is hard, if white folks give you a nickel or dime to get you somethin' to eat you has to write everything down in a book before you can get it. I always worked in the field, had to carry big logs, had strap on my arms and them logs was put in de strap and hauled to a pile where they all was. One morning it was rainin' and I didn't want to go to the field, but the overseer he come and got me and started whipping me. I jumped on him and bit and kicked him 'til he let me go. I didn't know no better then.

But Marster Lucas give us big times on Christmas and July. Us would have big dinners and all the lemonade us could drink. The dinner'd be spread out on the ground and all the niggers would stand roun' and eat all they wanted. What was left us'd take it to our cabins. Nancy Lucas was the cook for everybody. Well, she'd sure cook good cake and had plenty of them but she wouldn't like to cut them cakes often. She keep them in a safe. One day I go to that safe and I seen some and I wanted it to bad til I just had to have some. Nancy say to me, "Martha, did you cut that cake?" I say, "No sir! that knife just flew 'roun by itself and cut that cake."

One day I was workin' in the field and the overseer he come 'roun and say something to me he no business say. I took my hoe and knocked him plum down. I knowed I'se done somethin' bad so I run to the bushes. Marster Lucas come and got me and started whippin' me. I say to Marster Lucas what that overseer say to me and Marster Lucas didn' hit me no more. Marse Lucas was always good to us and he wouldn' let nobody run over his niggers.

There was plenty white folks that was sure bad to the niggers, and specially them overseers. A nigger what lived on the plantation joinin' ours shot and killed an overseer; then he run away. He come to the river and seen a white man on the other side and say, "Come and get me." Well, when they got him they found out what he'd done and was going to burn him alive. Judge Clements, the man that keep law and order, say he wouldn't burn a dog alive, so he left. But they sure burn that nigger alive for I seen him after he was burned up.

Us'd go to meetin' to the Antioch Church some Sundays. Us'd go to the house and get a pass. When us'd pass by the patterole (patrol), us just hold up our pass and then us'd go on. There was a 'vidin' [dividing] 'twixt the niggers and the white folks. The white preacher'd preach; then the colored man. Us'd stay at church most all day. When we didn't go to church, us'd get together in the quarters and have reachin' and singin' amongst ourselves.

In cotton pickin' time us'd stay in the field til way after dark and us'd pick by candle light and then carry it and put it on de scaffold. In the winter time us'd quilt; just go from one house to another in the quarter. Us'd weave all our everyday clothes, get us dresses and shoes and we'd sure be proud of them.

In slavery time they doctored the sick folks different from what they does now. I seen a man so sick they had to put medicine down his throat like he was a horse. That man got well and sure lived to turn a key in the jail. If it was in these days that man would be carried to the hospital and cut open like a hog.

There was a slave what live in Macon county. He run away and when he was caught they dug a hole in the ground and laid him across it and beat him nigh to death.

Source Notes

1. Henry Trumbull, *Life and Adventures of Robert. The Hermit of Massachusetts, Who has lived 14 Years in a Cave, secluded from human society, comprising An account of his Birth, Parentage, Sufferings, and providential escape from unjust and cruel Bondage in early life—and his reasons for becoming a Recluse. Taken from his own mouth, and published for his benefit.* Providence: Printed for H. Trumbull, 1829.

2. Mary Prince, *The History of Mary Prince. A West Indian Slave. Written by Herself.* London: F. Westley and A. H. Davis, 1831.

3. "The Beautiful Slave," in *The Colored American.* New York, July 8, 1837.

4. Josiah Henson, "Truth Is Stranger Than Fiction," *An Autobiography of the Rev. Josiah Henson.* Boston: B. B. Russell & Co., 1879.

5. Solomon Northup, *Twelve Years A Slave. Narrative of Solomon Northup, A Citizen of New-York, Kidnapped in Washington City in 1841, and Rescued in 1853, From a Cotton*

Plantation near the Red River in Louisiana. Auburn: Derby and Miller, Buffalo: Derby, Orton and Mulligan, Cincinnati: Henry W. Derby, 1853.

6. Ibid.

7. *Aunt Sally; or, The Cross the Way to Freedom. Narrative of the Slave-Life and Purchase of the Mother of Rev. Isaac Williams, of Detroit, Michigan.* Cincinnati: American Reform Tract and Book Society, 1858.

8. Rev. H. Mattison, M.A. *Louisa Picquet, The Octoroon: A Tale of Southern Life.* New York: The author, 1861.

9. Harriet Jacobs (Linda Brent), *Incidents in the Life of A Slave Girl. Written by Herself.* Edited by L. Maria Child. Boston: Published for the author, 1861.

10. Dr. L. S. Thompson, *The Story of Mattie J. Jackson; Her Parentage—Experience of Eighteen Years in Slavery—Incidents During the War—Her Escape From Slavery. A True Story. Written and Arranged by Dr. L. S. Thompson (Formerly Mrs. Schuyler), as Given By Mattie.* Lawrence, Kan.: Printed at Sentinel Office, 1866.

11. Elizabeth Keckley, *Behind the Scenes. Or, Thirty Years a Slave and Four Years in the White House.* New York: G.W. Carleton & Co., 1868.

12. Sarah H. Bradford, *Harriet. The Moses of Her People.* New York: George R. Lockwood & Son, 1886.

13. Bethany Viney, *The Narrative of Bethany Viney, A Slave Woman.* Worcester, Mass.: n.p., 1890.

14. The Ohio Project, the Schomburg Collection of the New York Public Library. Published by the U.S. Government.

Bibliography

Aunt Sally; or, The Cross the Way to Freedom. Narrative of the Slave-Life and Purchase of the Mother of Rev.Isaac Williams, of Detroit, Michigan. Cincinnati: American Reform Tract and Book Society, 1858.

Botkin, B. A., ed. *Lay My Burden Down. A Folk History of Slavery.* Chicago: University of Chicago Press, 1945.

Bell, Bernard Bell. *The Afro-American Novel and Its Tradition.* Amherst: University of Massachusetts Press, 1987.

Bradford, Sarah H. *Harriet. The Moses of Her People.* New York: George R. Lockwood & Son, 1886.

Delaney, Lucy A. *From the Darkness Cometh the Light; or, Struggles for Freedom.* St. Louis, Mo.: Publishing House of J. T. Smith, n.d.

Foster, Frances Smith. *Written by Herself: Literary Production by African American Women, 1746-1892.* Bloomington: Indiana University Press, 1993.

Gilbert, Olive. *Narrative of Sojourner Truth: A Bondswoman of Olden Time, Emancipated by the New York Legislature in the Early Part of the Present Century*. Boston: Published for the author, 1875.

Jacobs, Harriet (Linda Brent). *Incidents in the Life of A Slave Girl. Written by Herself.* Edited by L. Maria Child. Boston: Published for the author, 1861.

Hurmence, Belinda, ed. *My Folks Don't Want Me to Talk about Slavery. Twenty-one Oral Histories of Former North Carolina Slaves*. Winston-Salem, N.C.: John F. Blair, 1984.

Kaplan, Sidney. *The Black Presence in the Era of the American Revolution. 1770-1800*. Washington, D.C.: Smithsonian Institution Press, 1973.

Keckley, Elizabeth. *Behind the Scenes. Or, Thirty Years a Slave and Four Years in the White House*. New York: G.W. Carleton & Co., 1868.

Larison, Cornelius W., M.D. *Silvia DuBois, A Biography of the Slave Who Whipt Her Mistress and Gand Her Freedom*. Reprint. New York: Oxford University Press, 1988.

Lee, Jarina. *Religious Experience and Journal of Mrs. Jarina Lee, Giving an Account of Her Call to Preach the Gospel*. Philadelphia: The author, 1849.

Mattison, Rev. H., M.A. *Louisa Picquet, The Octoroon: A Tale of Southern Life*. New York: The author, 1861.

McDougall, F. H. *Memoirs of Eleanor Eldridge*. Providence, R.I.: B. T. Albro Printer, 1838.

Memoir of Old Elizabeth, A Colored Woman; With A Short Account of Her Last Sickness and Death. Philadelphia: Collins, Printer, 1866.

Northup, Solomon. *Twelve Years A Slave. Narrative of Solomon Northup, A Citizen of New-York, Kidnapped in Washington City in 1841, and Rescued in 1853, From a Cotton Plantation near the*

Red River in Louisiana. Auburn: Derby and Miller, Buffalo: Derby, Orton and Mulligan, Cincinnati: Henry W. Derby, 1853.

Prince, Mary. *The History of Mary Prince. A West Indian Slave. Written by Herself.* London: F. Westley and A. H. Davis, 1831.

Prince, Nancy. *A Narrative of the Life and Travels of Mrs. Nancy Prince. Written by Herself.* Boston: The author, 1853.

Thompson, Dr. L.S. *The Story of Mattie J. Jackson; Her Parentage—Experience of Eighteen Years in Slavery—Incidents During the War—Her Escape From Slavery. A True Story. Written and Arranged by Dr. L.S. Thompson (Formerly Mrs. Schuyler). As Given By Mattie.* Lawrence, Kan.: Printed at Sentinel Office, 1866.

Trumbull, Henry. *Life and Adventures of Robert. The Hermit of Massachusetts, Who has lived 14 Years in a Cave, secluded from human society, comprising An account of his Birth, Parentage, Sufferings, and providential escape from unjust and cruel Bondage in early life—and his reasons for becoming a Recluse. Taken from his own mouth, and published for his benefit.* Providence: Printed for H. Trumbull, 1829.

Viney, Bethany. *The Narrative of Bethany Viney, A Slave Woman.* Worcester, Mass.: n.p., 1890.

Wilson, Marion Starling. *The Slave Narrative. Its Place in American History.* Washington, D.C.: Howard University Press, 1988.

Suggested Reading

Albert, Octavia V. *The House of Bondage, or Charlotte Brooks and Other Slaves*. New York: Oxford University Press, 1988.

Burton, Annie L. *Memories of Childhood's Slavery Days*. Boston, 1919.

Clayton, Ronnie W. *Mother Wit: The Ex-slave Narratives of the Louisiana Writer's Project*. N.Y.: P. Lang, 1990.

Curtin, Phillip, ed. *Africa Remembered; Narratives by West Africans from the Era of the Slave Trade*. Madison, Wisc.: University of Wisconsin Press, 1967.

Dormigold, Kate. *A Slave Girl's Story, The Autobiography of Kate Dormigold* [sic]. Brooklyn, N.Y., 1898.

Foster, Frances Smith. *Witnessing Slavery; the Development of Ante-bellum Slave Narratives*. Westport, Conn.: Greenwood Press, 1979.

Lerna, Gerda, ed. *Black Women in White America*. New York: Vintage Books, 1973.

Mellon, James, ed. *Bullwhip Days: the Slaves Remember*. New York: Weidenfeld and Nicholson, 1988.

Nichols, Charles Harold. *Many Thousands Gone; the Ex-slaves' Account of their Bondage and Freedom*. Leiden: Brill, 1963.

Six Women's Slave Narratives. New York: Oxford University Press, 1989.

Thomas, James P. *From Tennessee Slave to St. Louis Entrepreneur*. Columbia: University of Missouri Press, 1984.

Index

109